# DATE DUE

|  |  |  |  |
|---|---|---|---|
|  |  |  |  |
|  |  |  |  |
|  |  |  |  |
|  |  |  |  |
|  |  |  |  |
|  |  |  |  |
|  |  |  |  |
|  |  |  |  |
|  |  |  |  |
|  |  |  |  |
|  |  |  |  |
|  |  |  |  |
|  |  |  |  |
|  |  |  |  |
|  |  |  |  |
|  |  |  |  |
|  |  |  |  |
|  |  |  | PRINTED IN U.S.A. |

# DO IT NOW

**Dr. William J. Knaus**, a psychologist–psychotherapist, is the director of the Fort Lee (New Jersey) Consultation Center and has an active private practice in New York City and Springfield, Massachusetts. Dr. Knaus has previously served as a professor on the staffs of the City University of New York, Pace University, and Southampton College of Long Island University, and as a post-doctoral fellow at Teachers College, Columbia University. He formerly directed the training of post-graduate psychotherapists at the Institute for Rational-Emotive Living, New York City. His articles and books on psychology emphasize strategies for improving the psychological functioning of adults, adolescents, and children.

# DO IT NOW

# HOW TO STOP PROCRASTINATING

## DR. WILLIAM J. KNAUS

PRENTICE
HALL
PRESS

New York    London    Toronto    Sydney    Tokyo    Singapore

**Prentice Hall Press**
15 Columbus Circle
New York, New York 10023

Copyright © 1979 by Prentice Hall Press
A Division of Simon & Schuster, Inc.

Published in 1986 by Prentice Hall Press
Originally published by Prentice-Hall, Inc.
Illustrations by Don Martinetti

PRENTICE HALL PRESS and colophons are registered
trademarks of Simon & Schuster Inc.

*Library of Congress Cataloging-in-Publication Data*

Knaus, William J.
Do it now.

Bibliography: p.
Includes index.
1. Self-actualization (Psychology)   2. Procrastina-
tion.   I. Title.
BF637.S4K56     158′.1     78-26631
ISBN 0-13-216606-2 pbk.

Manufactured in the United States of America

21   20   19   18   17

*Dedicated to
Wilbert and Catherine Knaus,
my father and mother.*

# Contents

# 16

# Foreword

Procrastination devastatingly affects many lives. But there are many effective methods currently available to change devastating procrastination patterns. Dr. Bill Knaus has been actively developing such methods for more than ten years and his major work has come to fruition in this timely book, which holds great promise of help for even the most inveterate procrastinator.

Fortunately, there are many ways to examine the problem, and there are multiple ways to counter the problem. The awareness–action approach advanced in Dr. Knaus's book is in the tradition he had established with his highly successful preventive mental-health approach for children and adolescents, *Rational Emotive Education*. Thus it contains ways to be aware of or to identify: the procrastination habit, the underlying dynamics, and action methods to get rid of the problem.

This means that serious persons wishing to rid themselves of procrastination have a well-guided pathway that can enable them to reach the point where they control the problem rather than be controlled by the procrastination habit.

To discover more, read the pages within. I'll write no more so that you can quickly begin.

L. René Gaiennie, Ph.D.
Senior Vice President,
Singer Company (ret.)
Fellow,
American Psychological Association

# Preface

The popular term describing unnecessary delays is *procrastination*. Procrastination, at one time or other, negatively affects virtually everyone. Fortunately, there are many ways for developing skills for eliminating such delays and for "getting it done." This book describes many tested approaches designed to help the reader achieve this end.

This book can be helpful to persons directly struggling to develop their ability and skills to effectively do it now. The methods contained within can also be helpful to mental-health counselors and those training to be counselors who are interested in learning ways to help their clients deal with the sort of procrastination difficulties outlined in this work.

*Do It Now* grew out of my personal contribution to an earlier book, *Overcoming Procrastination*, co-written with Albert Ellis. In this current effort, I have attempted to present a theory of the dynamics underlying procrastination, fresh ideas on how to stop procrastinating, and a new and much-needed program of concrete activities and exercises that can be used to deal with the procrastination problem.

In my opinion, all good therapists work to aid clients in developing awareness and action skills. This work presents well-tested methods to develop these skills. Sometimes, developing awareness and action skills requires the temporary help of a *trained* and *skilled* therapist. The materials contained herein, however, may provide for the serious "self helper" all the assistance necessary.

*Do It Now* comes theoretically closest to cognitive-behavior therapy in its orientation. Cognitive-behavior therapy is a psychotherapeutic methodology that represents a synthesis of action-oriented systems, such as behavior therapy, behavior modification, and rational-emotive psychotherapy. Cognitive-behavior therapists emphasize helping people to improve their ability to effectively function through teaching them to identify their strengths and to use their strengths constructively. To this end, cognitive-behavior clients learn to change maladaptive beliefs and attitudes and self-defeating behaviors.

*Do It Now* additionally incorporates insight principles from neo-analytic work by Heinz Hartman, Alfred Adler, and Karen Horney. Some of its concepts derive from the work of Gestalt, personal construct, client-centered, general semantic, and attribution theorists and clinical practitioners. *Do It Now*, however, emphasizes rational-emotive therapy principles and mainly my own personal theories developing out of my work with thousands of people who call themselves procrastinators.

I have organized my own work and the work of other insight and action systems according to an awareness-and-action format.

Thus, this work represents an attempt to organize awareness-and-action concepts and activities in a systematic, comprehensive, and helpful fashion. To assist readability of the text, I have kept the citing of references to a minimum; however, for the more academically inclined, I have included a modest bibliography that can be used as a jumping-off point for additional study on the topic of systems and methods that can be adapted in coping with procrastination.

This book builds upon awareness-and-action concepts that have been tested either in clinical experiments or through my own clinical practice. In this practice I have worked with many people desiring to overcome procrastination and shared in their struggle to push aside blocks to the pathway to progress. In this work I have found no universally effective method. What I have found is that those who are receptive to learning about themselves and are willing to change can almost always be helped to find a way or ways to do both. Incorporated in this book are the approaches to building awareness-and-action skills my clients have found most helpful and effective.

# Acknowledgments

I would like to acknowledge Albert Ellis, Edward Garcia, Jon Geis, Nancy Haberstroh Knaus, and especially L. René Gaiennie, who in one way or another influenced the development of this work.

I also would like to thank Lynne Lumsden and Thomas Coates, whose suggestions and recommendations at the critical early phase of this work were most helpful and encouraging.

Finally, I would like to thank my editor, Eric Newman, for his fine help and conscientious effort in guiding the manuscript toward its becoming a book.

# Introduction

*Do It Now* is an awareness-and-action book that espouses the position so well expressed by Emmanuel Kant—experience without theory is blind, but theory without experience is a mere intellectual play. This book, therefore, is designed to help you:

1. develop an awareness of the foundation to your procrastination problem
2. identify workable action solutions to overcoming procrastination

With awareness-and-action solutions firmly in mind, your task is to get the experience dealing with the procrastination problem and perhaps evolve theories of your own from these experiences.

Thoreau once said that for every thousand persons hacking at the branches of evil, only one person chops at its roots. Unfortunately, most people who procrastinate tend to chop at the branches (the individual acts of procrastionation) rather than attack the roots of the problem. *Do It Now* is also designed to help the reader to boil the problem down to its basic elements; and the reader can then gain an advantage in getting it done because his efforts can be directed right at the heart of the problem.

The awareness-and-action approach taken in this book helps the reader analyze the procrastination problem and to use this problem analysis to develop workable solutions for acting without needless delay. This problem analysis involves identifying procrastination patterns, and the mental myths or harmful misconceptions that support a procrastination pattern of which the person may be unaware.

*Do It Now* can aid the reader to conceptually identify, clarify, and undermine faulty thinking patterns that culminate in undesirable and self-defeating behavioral delays. The beginning portion of this book particularly emphasizes ways to become aware and to conceptually change.

In conjunction with a program emphasizing conceptual change, this book equally spotlights behavioral methods that are designed to help the reader act the way he would like to act. Unlike awareness, which is developed, action is initiated. So this focus is upon the actions that can be initiated that have a high probability of helping to get it done effectively. When a person acts effectively, I find his mental outlook is often improved. Such improvement can lead to an escalation of self-benefiting actions, and those actions to more productive and creative awarenesses.

In this growth process, the person trying to change procrastination patterns may delightfully find progress to be rapid. At times, however, changing actions will be slow and frustrating. During such phases, I suggest pausing and trying to identify what the bottlenecks are, and then conscienciously acting to overcome them.

Bottlenecks are not always psychological. At times, one's physical condition can hamper even the best intentions. If one is in the grips of the flu, suffers from a severe headache, or a temporary hormonal imbalance, efficiency will usually drop. After all, one is not a perpetual-motion machine! In addition to one's physical state, one may lack certain basic skills, such as how to organize, and thus will operate less efficiently. For example, when one first decides to work more arduously at administering the details of daily living, one will be less capable than later on when one has had considerable practice.

Speaking of work, this is not a book on how to enjoy tasks that are normally disliked. Admittedly, there are many mundane and unpleasant drudgeries in everyday life. When they are efficiently dispensed with, considerable time is freed for getting on with the business of pleasurable living.

*Do It Now* is structured to help you use your efforts productively to get on which the business of pleasurable living. It begins by suggesting a framework for understanding the roots of the problem, then shifts to a description of the basic distractions that obscure the roots from awareness. This concept of distraction is elaborated upon in Chapters 3, 4, 5, and 6, and each of these chapters includes exercises to help you to increase your skill in getting it done.

Since the need for comfort is so central in the process of understanding the roots of the problem and in changing procrastination patterns, Chapter 7 elaborates this concept and suggestions are provided for dealing with this problem.

The book's content shifts dramatically in Chapter 8 to provide a new and fresh slant on the procrastination problem through a description of procrastination styles and of strategies for combatting them.

Chapters 9, 10, and 11 are centered on themes of using objective thinking, creative imagination, and developing contact with real feelings to help you to mobilize for action. Chapters 12 and 13 continue with organizational and follow-through strategies to aid this momentum.

In Chapter 14, action-planning methods are spotlighted, and Chapter 15 extends this concept by describing how action planning and other antiprocrastination concepts can be combined and integrated into a master antiprocrastination plan. Finally, Chapter 16 suggests what life as a "getting it 'dunner' " could be like.

The structure of this book, in short, moves from general to increasingly specific ways to begin getting it done.

Specifically, this book includes hundreds of strategies, exercises, or hints for *doing it now*. Some methods you may find more relevant as aids to getting it done, so you are advised to concentrate your efforts more upon using those methods.

It is quite important to use the methods outlined in this book discriminatively and actively. Passively reading about how to get it done simply will not work. Test the exercises out—ACT!

Before embarking, I want to share some ideas from two great psychologists and educators; William James and John Dewey.

James proposes that the strength of will (the power to choose a goal or purpose and to direct attention to meet its requirements) is instrumental in achieving objectives. According to James's philosophy, getting it done would be a function of an exercise of will. In principle, procrastination is reduced by strengthening one's power to make appropriate choices (accomplished through education) and through the enactment of those choices.

In John Dewey's view, one procrastinates after establishing a goal, and, when instead of achieving daily objectives leading to attainment of the goal, one waits passively for the time to come when the goal will magically be achieved. One does not, in other words, fully involve oneself in the day to day process of working toward the goal. Predictably, Dewey's solution for overcoming procrastination was for a person to actively engage himself in the process of experiencing and experimenting. Dewey suggested that people develop motivation to overcome procrastination by participating in purposeful experience and action.

Both James and Dewey emphasize that effort is required to realize goals—a view I heartily endorse!

As you embark on your journey to reduce needless delay and to obtain greater satisfaction with living, I won't wish you luck. Instead, I wish you the will to persevere and to experience the good sweat of accomplishment. In this process, I wish you more than desire to beat this problem; I wish you the courage to try.

# 1

# Stop Fiddling and Start Doing

"At the beginning, there was much to do, but by whittling away, the tasks became few."

Molly Martin and Bob Beaver, two animal therapists, decided to organize a workshop for the forest animals on the topic of procrastination. Procrastination, the habit of putting off until tomorrow what is uncomfortable to do today, was a major problem plaguing most of the forest animals. Molly and Bob knew that getting it done really could leave more time for having fun, so they decided to entitle the workshop "Get It Done and Still Have Fun."

1

There were many likely candidates for the workshop. Randy Rabbit was one. Randy was deeply troubled after his loss in a race against a country turtle. In fact, he felt quite depressed these days and found himself putting off applying for the job he wanted as a speedy runner for a messenger service. He was beginning to doubt if he could manage to keep the job if he were fortunate enough to be hired. Jill the grasshopper was next to register for the workshop. She had made it through the last winter by winning the local lottery, and lately, instead of fiddling, she was worrying about how she was going to store provisions before the winter without hassling herself too much in the process. Pringle Pig, of The Three Little Pigs fame, arrived with a sense of skepticism. He was all for having more fun. He wasn't sure about the "Get It Done" part of the workshop, however. Nevertheless, still badly shaken up over his close call with the local big bad wolf, he was coming to the conclusion that his previous life of "taking it easy" wasn't so easy after all.

As usual, as Randy, Jill, Pringle, and the other workshop participants were about to begin with Molly and Bob, Pat Cat and Sally Crow were still deliberating whether to join. Finally, the group began without them, so Pat turned to Sally and said, "Maybe we ought to wait until the workshop is given next year. That will give us more time to prepare for it."

The procrastination problems of the animal workshop group represent only a small portion of the sort of procrastination problems people have. So we'll leave the forest workshop to Molly and Bob and begin with our own self-help program. We will begin by considering what this book will help you to accomplish.


## AWARENESS

People today are steeped in consciousness raising. We are confronted with all sorts of movements aimed at making us *aware*. One purpose of this book, likewise, is to help you to become aware of *how* you procrastinate. A second purpose is to help you to decide *what* you can do to take action to *get it done*. In both endeavors it is

my intent to help you figure out and act upon ways to open new opportunities by *getting it done*.

People (and even Molly and Bob's animal-group members) have many styles of procrastinating, and by procrastinating, they avoid many types of opportunities. Regardless of the area of procrastination and the types of opportunities lost because of putting it off, people who procrastinate generally are optimistic that their problems will be easier to contend with in the future. They subscribe to a system of wishful thinking—fiddling away their present lives on what are often fruitless hopes of wonderful days to come. Unfortunately, this "better future" concept disguises the reality that procrastination patterns will not magically disappear some day in the future. As a result of this wishful thinking, the procrastination pattern thwarts both present and future happiness. Like the Beatles' Eleanor Rigby, the procrastinator simply "waits by the door."

Some delays, to be sure, are the result of a well-thought-through decision, and the person who waits by choice does not fit into the Eleanor Rigby category. So what are the reasons why people put things off?

## FIVE REASONS FOR DELAYS

There are five basic reasons for delays: physical incapacitation, ignorance, stratagem, discomfort dodging, and self-doubt. Physical incapacitation is when one has severe medical problems that serve to stop him or her from proceeding. Ignorance is when a person doesn't realize a deed needs doing: A person learning a new job may need time to develop awareness of the job's priorities. Some delays are strategic: The executive conducts a market survey before committing money and resources to develop a soap that will be competitive on the market; or a young woman wants to get to know a new acquaintance before accepting his proposal of marriage. The delays due to physical causes, ignorance, or strategy are understood and accepted. The form of delays we will consider in this book are needless delays—ones that interfere with both psychological growth and the smooth administration of life's details, the ones created by discomfort dodging and self-doubt. Both are the result of erroneous perceptions that you can work to change.

Knowing the two major psychological problems tied to procrastination makes it possible for one to go directly to the source of the procrastination problem. The advantage of being able to identify these two contributing dynamic forces provides one with enormous advantage in efficiently getting to the heart of the problem. So with this in mind, let's examine discomfort dodging and self-doubt.

## Discomfort Dodging

As in the case of the snake phobic who fears the woods out of an exaggerated fear of being bitten by a snake, faulty, misguided thinking occurs in discomfort dodging. In discomfort dodging, the task, like the walk in the woods, is put off because some parts of it are associated with uncomfortable, possibly anxious, feelings. Thus in discomfort dodging the goal is to avoid feeling bad. But discomfort dodging is like a mental pollutant that colors inconveniences and makes them seem more weighty and difficult than they actually are.

When any unpleasant but important activity is avoided because the person wants to avoid hassle, this is termed *discomfort dodging*. Discomfort dodging can intensify to the point that even enjoyable activities are avoided because of certain hassles associated with their preparations. For example, you may think roller-skating is enjoyable but find the steps involved in getting to do it (dressing, putting the skates on) too much of a hassle, and thus a reason not to go.

I find that people who procrastinate are often finely attuned to their psychophysical sensations of comfort and discomfort (they are "sensation-suggestive"). So if they anticipate feeling uncomfortable, they will feel physical sensations of discomfort that they will interpret as a signal to avoid the anticipated source of discomfort. That is why some people, on a warm day at the seashore, resist jumping in the water and going swimming. They "blow up," in their minds, the momentary discomfort of feeling cold before their bodies adjust to the temperature change. Yet once in the water, the same people are inclined to remark to themselves, "The water isn't really as cold as I thought; in fact, the water is quite pleasant." So it seems that often the resistance in the doing is a result of stewing about the doing.

Practice discomfort dodging and the tendency gets stronger. Practice can culminate in an outcome in which small inconveniences, such as writing a letter of recommendation for a colleague, are routinely put aside. What is dangerous about this practice is that small inconveniences tend to be forgotten and piled up, remembered, put off again, remembered again, and finally completed far too late or permanently put aside.

### Self-doubt

Self-doubt is another changeable attitude that often leads to self-deprecation and procrastination. People who suffer from self-doubt have a deficiency outlook and are preoccupied with their faults. This preoccupation substitutes for creativity and productivity, and the absence of these two qualities opens the pathway to procrastination.

Self-doubt occurs when a person judges his abilities as questionable and defines his adequacy as a person on the basis of those questionable qualities. Doubting one's abilities can lead to self-downing, a sense of worthlessness, and procrastination. So if a person doubts his ability to make friends, he can "down" himself for this presumed "defect," put off trying to make friends, and then down himself for having few friends.

Self-doubt need not lead to self-downing and procrastination. One can be unsure of one's artistic talent as a painter and take a college course to see if one can develop the skill. Generally, however, among people who procrastinate, self-doubt leads to a self-downing sequence that is part of a procrastination syndrome.

Self-doubt is relative. One can wake up feeling confident and later feel, for no obvious reason, unworthy and forlorn—and experience this feeling in varying degrees. This attitude of self-doubt exists on a continuum. The range is from a sense of full self-confidence to a sense of utter worthlessness. Thus one's place on the continuum can fluctuate according to mood or situation. For example, let's say a normally self-confident person attempts to learn a complicated new game and studies with a teacher who is harshly critical. This person, who typically feels confidence, finds himself making continual errors and becomes temporarily preoccupied with thoughts of how stupid he is. At the opposite end of the continuum, a normally self-doubting person may color his life with self-debasing ideas interspersed with only brief moments of self-confidence. Thus self-doubt may also be relatively constant. Normally, a more intensely negative self-view is closely associated with hesitating and delaying; a positive self-view is closely associated with an orientation toward seeking opportunity, persistence, and purposefulness.

Sometimes a person who is riddled with self-doubts and who hates discomfort works despite fear because the consequences of giving up or of procrastinating are thought to be too uncomfortable to bear—a loss of prestige, a crack in the ideal image, or a fear of public censure. So this person runs to avoid failure and obscures opportunity in this mad dash. While people generally change through taking action, this is the exception. Repetitive and driven actions (sometimes termed work-aholism) obscure opportunity because the person's eyes are on escape and his energies are dissipated in this pursuit. (We'll return to consider this diversionary ploy in the next chapter, under the heading "Action Diversions.")

## MIXED BAG

Discomfort dodging and self-doubt have been discussed independently, but in real life they are typically integrated. Generally, both self-doubt and discomfort dodging are the result of interwoven patterns of self-defeating attitudes. These attitudes, like dragons of the spirit, plague the mind and block energies. And when these two attitudes rule together, they reciprocally retard advancement. Self-doubt is an uncomfortable feeling, and, existing in a person who wishes to dodge discomfort, becomes a signal of inability to control one's thoughts and feelings. This in turn leads to more uncomfortable feelings of inadequacy. (This conflict is like stopping one's automobile at each branch of a road with one foot pressing hard on the brake pedal and the other on the accelerator, waiting to make a decision as to which foot to release or in which direction to travel.) This process continues until one feels numb or something happens to distract one from this pattern (falling asleep, blaming someone else, a phone call, starting work). Obviously, so long as the person is caught in this reciprocal cycle the norm is "stewing rather than doing." But unlike one's fingerprints, which do not change, attitudes—even discomfort dodging and self-doubting—can be changed.

Self-doubt and discomfort dodging are attitudes (evaluations) and as such are subject to the laws of learning. These self-defeating, procrastination-creating attitudes are learned and can be countered by new learnings. One new learning is to consistently take advantage of opportunity. This getting-it-done pattern can displace procrastination and can be accomplished by allowing oneself to (1) *plan* for attaining what is desired and *follow* the plan; (2) work to destroy the problem at its source (self-doubt and discomfort dodging); (3) learn and apply logical techniques of objective evaluation (described later); (4) actively engage normally put-off projects. Furthermore, since there is a strong interrelationship among self-doubt, discomfort dodging, and procrastination, changes in one lead to changes in the other two.

You can learn methods to stop procrastinating, increase self-confidence, and increase tolerance for discomfort. When you do, there are at least two enormously worthwhile benefits. One is the feeling of satisfaction gained by completing work promptly. The second, perhaps greater benefit is the development of emotional freedom: Just imagine having worry-free time to savor life. Once you are clear of the unhappy procrastination habit, imagine maintaining the power to experience a sense of accomplishment and the stable feeling of self-acceptance.

The purpose of this chapter is to raise your awareness of procrastination and its psychological foundations. Awareness is a useful, although not necessarily sufficient, condition for change. To change you have to alter your actions as well as your outlook. You can use the following activities to heighten your awareness and get into action. The following activities provide guidelines you can use to carefully define the limits of procrastination, identify goals for change, and identify strategies for change.

## EXERCISES FOR CHANGE

An important step in getting it done is developing skill in self-observation. Self-observation involves learning to become objectively aware of yourself—what you value, what you think, what you feel, and what you do.

One helpful way of teaching yourself to be a more astute self-observer is to buy a notebook and maintain a log of your activities. Using a notebook to objectively record what you are doing and what you are thinking and feeling makes it easier to be more factually aware of "where you are at" and aware of your progress over time. Also, having a notebook makes it convenient to record plans and scratch out plans you want to change as well as to add new ideas. In short, the notebook can provide a central storage file for information you can use in your antiprocrastination campaign (or, more positively stated, your "getting it done" campaign).

This first series of exercises is designed to help you to heighten your awareness of what you tend to put off, and to organize this information such that it can be used not only to serve as an aid for identifying priorities, but also to help you target in on basic underlying problems that you can work toward eliminating.

As a first step in this process of identifying problem areas complete the Procrastination Inventory, which follows. It can help you to isolate those areas in which you procrastinate.

# PROCRASTINATION INVENTORY

Complete this inventory by citing examples from your life that support or refute each item. Then, based upon your own written testimony, place a check in the column (R=Rarely; O=Occasionally; SO=Somewhat Often; VF=Very Frequently) that you believe best summarizes your written description.

## Sample

| Problem | Evidence | Summary | | | |
|---|---|---|---|---|---|
| | | R | O | SO | VF |
| I delay until the eleventh hour before beginning important projects. | Reports generally started near deadline; pay taxes late; made travel arrangements four consecutive times just before the deadline; put antifreeze in car just before first freeze. | | | | |

Please complete the inventory with the view toward presenting a fair picture of yourself.

| Problem | Evidence | Summary | | | |
|---|---|---|---|---|---|
| | | R | O | SO | VF |
| 1. I delay until the eleventh hour before beginning important projects. | | | | | |
| 2. I believe I have too little to say to new acquaintances and shy away from meeting new people. | | | | | |
| 3. I like a routine life and try to follow the same daily pattern. | | | | | |

| | | | | | | |
|---|---|---|---|---|---|---|
| 4. I remain angry for long periods of time contemplating how I will take revenge on an adversary. | | | | | | |
| 5. I feel like a terrible person. | | | | | | |
| 6. I feel overwhelmed. | | | | | | |
| 7. I believe I won't be able to change the unpleasant way I feel. | | | | | | |
| 8. I can't stand inconveniences. | | | | | | |
| 9. I forecast disaster for myself and/or others. | | | | | | |
| 10. I become impatient when stuck in traffic or when I have to wait in line. | | | | | | |
| 11. I fail to return phone calls. | | | | | | |
| 12. I try to control others' behavior through guilt. | | | | | | |
| 13. I find myself acting indecisively. | | | | | | |
| 14. I pay bills late. | | | | | | |
| 15. I live my life in a state of disorganization. | | | | | | |

11

| | R | O | SO | VF |
|---|---|---|---|---|
| 16. I show up late for appointments. | | | | |
| 17. I repeat patterns I want to change. | | | | |
| 18. I hold back expressing what I feel. | | | | |
| 19. I feel embarrassed when I am with a friend who is acting foolishly. | | | | |
| 20. I collect materials to use on a project and then delay doing the project. | | | | |
| 21. I avoid situations where I believe I won't be very successful. | | | | |
| 22. I delay sending out correspondence. | | | | |
| 23. I buy gifts at the eleventh hour. | | | | |
| 24. I dwell upon how unjust the world is. | | | | |
| 25. I feel as though there is just one crisis after another in my life. | | | | |

| # | Statement | | | | | |
|---|-----------|---|---|---|---|---|
| 26. | I repeatedly replay arguments in my head. | ✓ | | | | |
| 27. | I daydream of accomplishing great feats. | ✓ | | | | |
| 28. | I tell myself that tomorrow I'll begin. | | | | | |
| 29. | I indulge my desire to avoid doing anything that is an inconvenience or a hassle. | ✓ | | | | |
| 30. | I worry that other people do not like me. | | | | | |
| 31. | I hate to deprive myself and thus indulge in that extra dessert or snack. | | | | | |
| 32. | I feel I have to have the last word in an argument. | | | | | |
| 33. | I become angry with myself when I can't seem to control my feelings. | | | | ✓ | |
| 34. | I make promises to myself or others that I put off keeping. | | | | | |
| 35. | I feel bored. | | | | | ✓ |
| 36. | I feel that I lack drive or energy. | | | | | ✓ |

13

This inventory surveys some areas that you may not have associated with procrastination. For example, items four and five may appear to have little to do with procrastination. However, time spent in vengeful or self-debasing contemplation robs time from involvement in self-fulfilling activities. So such items may suggest to you reasons why you stop yourself from being a more powerful and effective human being, and why you may procrastinate. The following items also fall into this diagnostic category: 7, 8, 9, 24, 26, 27, 30, and 33. On items like 35 and 36, if you checked Somewhat Often or Very Frequently, that may suggest that you avoid challenging yourself. Items like 3, 12, 17, and 33 if checked Somewhat Often or Very Frequently, may mean that you are trying too hard to keep in control and are thereby putting off developing flexibility.

This inventory can be interpreted or used in many different ways. So regardless of whether you decide to cluster items together to identify a pattern or examine each item separately, fear not, this book contains many strategies concerning how each inventoried item can be dealt with.

Although there are many ways the inventory can be interpreted, its main purpose is to heighten your awareness of potential procrastination trouble spots. I recommend that you use it in the following ways:

- to identify general trouble spots warranting your attention.

- to identify specific incidents in which procrastination is likely to erupt (from the "Evidence" section of the inventory).

- to assess the degree to which procrastination and problems related to procrastination pervade your life.

- to provide data you can refer to and use in the many exercises suggested throughout this book.

- for pre- and post-program comparisons so that you can assess your progress.

Items that you check as Somewhat Often or Frequent may be priority items that you especially desire to give special attention to in creating a getting-it-done program.

When you procrastinate, you may maintain your environment in ineffectual ways or minimize the development of your psychological potential. Poor maintenance results in problems such as undone household chores (cleaning, washing, paying bills); accumulations of outdated newspapers, magazines, or clothing; misplaced and lost materials; and delayed communications. Procrastinating on self-development is the same as putting off learning methods of self-discovery, learning techniques of self-evaluation, or developing talents and good personal qualities.

Typically, putting off personal development involves failing to: deal with troublesome personal problems; break unwanted habits; advance career possibilities; persevere with a valued hobby or interest; improve communication skills; and tolerate the unpleasant elements that lie on the pathway to your goals.

Now, use the above framework and the Procrastination Inventory to identify some of your major procrastination patterns. First divide an 8-by-12-inch sheet of paper into four quarters. Call this your " 'What to Get Done' Inventory" (an example follows). Starting on the top left side, list the maintenance chores you typically put off; in the lower left quadrant, list those chores in their order of importance. Repeat this process on the right side of the sheet for the self-development activities you tend to put off.

You may change your priorities as you proceed. In the meanwhile, the list can help you to discover how extensive your procrastination problem is and to identify the areas you need to work on harder to change. The list can be helpful in yet another way. As you work to reduce the number of items on the list, you will be doing more than learning how to be more efficient. You are eliminating some of the underlying causes of procrastination at the same time.

Use the following outline to help yourself identify the relationship between the activities you put off and self-doubt and discomfort dodging.

```
┌─────────────────────────────────────────┐
│        "WHAT TO GET DONE" INVENTORY      │
│   SELF-MAINTENANCE    SELF-DEVELOPMENT   │
│                     │                    │
│                     │                    │
│                     │                    │
│                     │                    │
│                     │                    │
│                     │                    │
│          ───────────┴──────────          │
│              PRIORITIES                  │
│      1                  1                │
│      2                  2                │
│      3                  3                │
│      4                  4                │
│      5                  5                │
│      6                  6                │
│      7                  7                │
│                                          │
└─────────────────────────────────────────┘
```

Using the maintenance and development activities you listed, categorize each according to which concept appears most dominant: self-doubt, discomfort dodging, or mixed (the problem seems to contain strong elements of both self-doubt and discomfort dodging). Do this by taking a sheet of paper and dividing it into three columns. Call this your "Growth Inventory" (an example follows). Designate one column "Self-Doubt," the second "Discomfort Dodging," and the third "Mixed." (*Hint:* Maintenance procrastination frequently reflects discomfort dodging or mixed; developmental procrastination frequently reflects self-doubt or mixed.) Use the top half of the sheet to list the items, and the lower half to order them according to the most to least important (priorities).

This act of categorizing procrastination problems can be helpful in several ways. First, you are being honest with yourself in admitting to the problem and in making clear to yourself what your

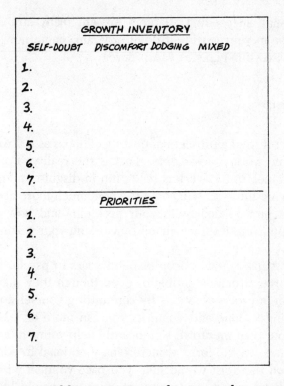

GROWTH INVENTORY

SELF-DOUBT   DISCOMFORT DODGING   MIXED

1.
2.
3.
4.
5.
6.
7.

PRIORITIES

1.
2.
3.
4.
5.
6.
7.

procrastination problems are. Second, your outline visually shows that whenever you work toward getting it done, you are creating opportunities to develop skills in acting more effectively and efficiently. Third, you are choosing growth over stagnation when you act to get it done. So when you take action, you are improving your skills in maintenance or fostering your psychological growth and you are reducing self-doubt, building self-confidence, and increasing tolerance for discomfort. To start the above process in motion, begin to work on a project now!

Pick a priority you have listed under one of your two listings (" 'What to Get Done' Inventory" and "Growth Inventory"). Take one step toward getting the task completed. When you have progressed, pick a second, and take a step toward eliminating that task. If your first selection was a maintenance project, make your second project a developmental project.

**17**

Although succeeding chapters present many strategies that you can use in your getting-it-done program, begin now. You can always revise your plans as you progress.

## POSTSCRIPT

Ironic, isn't it, that a problem of putting off looks as if it would take considerable work to overcome. That is the reality. Fortunately, however, much of the work is really fun in disguise, and, in addition to having fun, you will come to know much more about yourself, about how to deal with your problems and how to create positive opportunities for yourself by working your getting-it-done program.

Interestingly, many people spend years in psychotherapy to beat the procrastination problem, even though they may not call their problem procrastination. By committing yourself to work toward getting it done and doing it, you can more or less learn to become your own therapist, significantly help yourself, and collect your own fees in the form of increasing emotional freedom.

A good therapist would help you pace yourself wisely. Thus once you have begun to identify activities you would like to start getting done, it would be preferable to concentrate your efforts on one priority at a time. Try to avoid that feeling of being overwhelmed that comes from believing that all tasks are equally important and must be done all at once.

# Procrastination Practice

> "And those who were blind knew not of the elephant
> they touched."

There is an old proverb that says that one can't make a silk purse out of a sow's ear. Although the proverb is literally true, there are some people who can describe a sow's ear so that it *sounds* like the world's finest silk purse. We've all met such con artists who use gilded words with such aplomb that they can and do sell yellow bricks as gold and the Brooklyn Bridge as a high-quality investment. These are the masters of deceit, and they do their work well. In some ways there is an old con artist lurking under the

19

skin in most of us. And this wily part is sometimes so skillful in self-deception that the credibility of the self-con is seldom questioned.

The self-con works best when we render decisions that, in easing the burden of self-doubt, help us to dodge what we believe is uncomfortable. One such decision is to procrastinate. Of course, the person who decides to procrastinate doesn't apply that label to the decision. Instead, he decides to put off making a phone call or mopping the floor by gliding into some substitute activity like smoking, deciding that later is a better time to begin, or delaying until feelings of comfort and readiness prevail. Thus a decision that sounds like an action step is actually rendered to avoid acting. And the conscious or unconscious decision to divert from the less comfortable priority just serves to reinforce the procrastination habit.

Procrastination, like most habits, is resistant to change. This is because habits are not just isolated behaviors, but rather, tightly interwoven parts of the organizational structure of each person's psychological mosaic. Thus, each habit has to be seen in relationship to the totality of the person. Since procrastination is synonymous with a habit of needlessly delaying, it is important that we understand the nature of habits and then use this knowledge to see how procrastination fits into one's psychological mosaic and what can be done to remove the habit from that mosaic.

Habits are well-practiced routines that occupy a large portion of our daily lives while receiving little conscious recognition. If, for instance, you had to get up every morning and decide how to suds yourself in the shower or how to loop and tie your shoelaces, you'd be operating very slowly, and much mental energy would be exhausted before you even got out the door to go to work. Fortunately, you have developed a whole system of functional habits that allow you to concentrate on more productive thinking and acting.

The procrastination habit is as automatic as functional habits but serves the opposite effect—that of diverting from productive thinking and acting. This well-practiced procrastination/diversion routine or self-con is a clever distraction that creates a temporary sense of well-being.

Knowing the nature of these procrastination diversions can be extremely helpful in uprooting the problem. So in the remainder of this chapter I will describe the major procrastination diversions. Be warned, however: You may feel uncomfortable if you can associate one or more of these self-cons with your own actions. But unless you deal with these procrastination diversions, there is a danger that you will continue to use them. So the sooner you recognize and honestly and skillfully deal with the procrastination diversions, the sooner you will start getting more done. To help you in this effort, below I describe three major types of procrastination diversions, how to recognize them, and how to deal with them.

## ACTION DIVERSIONS

A person feels anxious about writing a report and finds chain-smoking, overeating, sleeping, playing solitaire, doing pushups—almost anything but doing the report—temporarily more rewarding. These activities are habitual responses to stress. They are *action diversions* because the person detours away from writing by engaging in substitute behaviors. Engrossed in the new activity, the would-be report writer temporarily seals off the feelings of anxiety, depression, or frustration he experiences in preparing to write. The person is now too busy thinking about the new diversion to worry about the work.

Action diversions or "addictivities" are frequently substituted for what must be done. Feeling discomfort at the prospect of tough work, work that could stimulate uncomfortable self-doubts, some people slide into these addictivities like a professional swimmer into water. The concrete problem—writing the report—is artfully dodged for the moment through absorption into the addictivity.

This process of artful dodging has many of the elements of the creative process. Both processes involve becoming absorbed in and committed to the activity. Thus, when one looks at two people who expend great amounts of energy and long hours in their work, they may appear similar, although one may be a "work-aholic" (artfully dodging facing a problem of inadequacy) and the other may be an artist, a teacher, or a businessperson who is finding a genuine means of expression through work and is creatively absorbed.

## SUGGESTIONS FOR OVERCOMING ADDICTIVITIES

If you know how you behaviorally divert yourself, you can start to change this pattern now!

- List your suspected addictivities (telephone, reading, smoking, cleaning).
- Identify the goals that these addictivities divert you from.
- Note *when* you are likely to employ diversion (e.g., "When I anticipate going to a social affair").

Now that the type of action diversion and circumstance are noted, *plan* to use future circumstances or the onset of the diversion as a *signal* to deal with the situation you are tempted to duck by using the following:

- You can rid yourself of addictivities through the constructive use of your powers of concentration. For example, habits are instantly broken when it is important enough to do so. Suppose you traveled to a country whose inhabitants drive on the opposite side of the road. If you decide to drive, you quickly adapt to the left side. You have that capacity and can use it even when your survival is not at stake. Try using these powers to do what you fear doing, taking a first step, then a second.
- Short-circuit pseudo-conflicts that impel action diversions. One such conflict is the "Should I or shouldn't I?" debate. The way this debate works is that one gets oneself anxious worrying about something such as one's popularity and then de-

velops an urge to eat all the cake in the refrigerator. Shortly thereafter, the diversionary conflict erupts in the form of "Should I or should I not eat the cake?" Then the "to eat or not to eat" conflict escalates to anxiety. And since it can appear that anxiety will continue as long as the cake is not eaten, the conflict is resolved by eating the cake. (It can also be resolved by throwing the cake into the garbage.) The conflict over eating the cake and the action of eating the cake has deflected the actor from the original and presumably painful problem (fear of not being popular and thereby being rejected). To short-circuit this process, try the following:

o Keep your eye on the original problem (in our example: popularity) and try to identify precisely what is bothering you. Try to articulate the problem to yourself; determine if the problem is largely real or largely imaginary; work at solving the problem.

o In order to disrupt the "Should I?" conflict, use a behavioral thought-stopping technique, such as internally screaming "STOP!" after each time you ask yourself "Should I?"

o Bear with the discomfort by making an agreement with yourself that you won't eat the cake (make the phone call, place a bet on the horses, argue with your spouse) for at least fifteen minutes and will decide after that time if you will go another fifteen minutes before engaging in the action diversion.

• Watch for the stage of self-seduction in which you give yourself appetizing reasons for engaging in the addictivity: "What is the harm?"; "It will feel good"; "Why deprive myself?"; "I deserve to have some pleasure." Make up a series of questions, like the following, that you ask yourself whenever you start to con yourself into the addictivity:

o What makes it so important for me to have to _____ (addictivity) right this minute?

   o Why do I need to feel good by_____?

                                (addictivity)

   o What other forms of pleasure can I have right now that will help me in the long run?

   o If I deserve to have some pleasure, why do I need the displeasure of the aftermath of_____?

                                (addictivity)

These questions can be written on a card, or you can tape-record them and play them back during an addictivity crisis.

- Use a paradoxical technique to exaggerate your situation. The technique is used to help you to build a healthy opposition to the addictivity, and not as a means of putting yourself down. The technique involves purposefully carrying on a dialogue with yourself along the following lines: "You poor soul. You really can't handle discomfort. You really have a good reason to doubt yourself because in truth you really are helpless to fight your urges. These urges are too big and strong for you to ignore—give in to them and keep giving in to them. Feel good for the moment. Your living in the moment is all that matters now. Don't look to the next moment. You won't be able to handle that one any better than you are handling this moment. So why bother trying?"

Keep up the dialogue for ten minutes.

- The night before an important examination, we find our procrastinating heroine busily consumed in reading her text in English grammar, going over her mistakes on the last examination. Unfortunately, she is scheduled to take an examination in biology and she has much to study in order to pass. Let's pause a moment to examine this example. In this case, the student is engaging in what I call a *switchover technique*. Switchover occurs when one shifts from one task to another. It can be very self-defeating (as in the above example), or it can be converted to a helpful activity. Switchover can be helpful if one agrees to spend only five minutes on the diversionary activity and then to use the momentum built up during that five minutes to switch over to the priority task.

Obviously, the purpose of these exercises is to deal with real problems and to open up opportunities. Paradoxically, if one loses sight of this intent, the exercises can serve as diversionary ploys.

## THE MAÑANA PRINCIPLES: MENTAL DIVERSIONS

Imagination can be a pregnant source for new ideas, but it can also be a mental vehicle for ducking the unpleasant. Clever creatures that we are, we sometimes use imagination for diversion. We can dodge problems through our intellectual processes, sometimes creating complex ways to think ourselves out of acting productively.

There are three major *mental diversions* to be aware of. All are cleverly deceptive—people are often unaware they use them. They are the *mañana*, the *contingency mañana*, and the *Catch-22 diversions*.

People con themselves into procrastinating by convincing themselves that they will get the uncomfortable task done tomorrow or some time soon. When tomorrow comes they tell themselves the same nonsense again. This is the mañana principle.

The mañana principle is a powerful form of self-deception because it enables a person to: (1) avoid admitting he or she is procrastinating; (2) avoid looking at the roots of the problem; (3) maintain a good image; and (4) feel hopeful. Underlying this principle is the assumption that "there is nothing wrong with delay since I'm not ready to begin now. Perhaps when I'm rested I'll begin. Perhaps later I'll have an easier time." Students (especially high-school students) are great adherents to this principle, particularly those who decide to put off their homework until they get home in preference to using the study-hall time for that purpose.

Here is the mañana principle in action: Albert would like to become a professional writer, but he is so afraid of failing that he does not even practice. When he thinks about writing professionally, he doesn't admit that he's afraid. Instead, he believes that he will start writing tomorrow, when he feels more rested.

A variation of the mañana principle is the practice of waiting for the "moment of inspiration." A person who believes he can work only when inspired temporarily eases tension by assuming work will be easier later because it will be done with inspiration. Unfortunately, "moments of inspiration" are rare and typically fizzle after a brief flourish of activity.

Another variation of the mañana principle is the contingency-mañana principle. *Contingent* means "dependent upon," and the contingency-mañana principle operates when a person makes completing an emotionally important project dependent upon completing a less important project first. Thus, unimportant, irrelevant, but deceptively credible preliminary tasks are given priority over the main activity. Now there are *two* things to procrastinate on—the substitute activity and the relevant activity. The substitute activity is conjured up because the main project is perceived as too threatening or uncomfortable to deal with directly.

The contingency-mañana principle is an important component of many procrastination problems. It is a subtle but powerful delaying tactic and is not easily recognized. The following examples illustrate how the principle works.

George procrastinated about establishing new friendships. First he excused himself by claiming that it wouldn't pay to try until he moved into a new apartment. After all, until then he wouldn't have a comfortable room in which to entertain his guests. When he moved into a new apartment (after six months' delay), he decided he had to furnish it lavishly before he could have visitors. After all, he couldn't have any prospective friends think he lived in barren surroundings. When George bought furniture, he discovered that he didn't have attractive curtains, so he then deluded himself into believing that he had to have the "right" curtains to entertain properly. He searched two months for the "right" curtains and then ordered curtains that wouldn't be delivered for six to eight weeks.

George points with pride to his preparatory accomplishments. He found a new apartment, moved in, bought new furniture, and ordered curtains. But by setting up his contingencies in this way, he delayed facing and resolving his fear that he would be unable to make friends.

George sets up preconditions or contingencies in order to cover up his fears. He believes he won't be able to establish friendships until his living environment is organized. He is actually secretly afraid that he won't do well in making friends even if his apartment were like that in a *House Beautiful* picture. Underlying this is the fear of rejection because of his personality, not his apartment. Thus, he detours his efforts from directly dealing with his basic problem to substituting activities.

The contingency mañana appears in many forms. Jack won't ask Suzie to marry him until he's "ready" (saved money, straightened out his head). "Somehow" he spends more than he earns and excuses himself from starting therapy because of the lack of financial resources. Jane won't write her dissertation on the sex habits of fireflies until she's sure that she has obtained and read all the literature on fireflies. She manages to avoid the library work because she thinks she doesn't know enough about how to do research and needs to read more on the topic.

Both the mañana and the contingency-mañana views create a false sense of decisiveness. These views imply a decision that today's problem will be remedied tomorrow or in the future some time, and when the mañana or contingency-mañana decision is made, the person may temporarily feel better because some action will be taken sometime. The self-con has worked, and the sow's ear once again has become a silk purse.

The Catch-22 diversion is similar to the contingency-mañana principle. In each case there is a condition that must be met before a primary project can be directly and actively dealt with. However, with the contingency mañana principle there is at least a theoretical chance to succeed. But with the Catch-22 ploy there is no chance. This is how it works.

In the novel *Catch-22*, the character Yossarian wanted to get out of the army. The only way to get out was to be adjudged crazy, but if he claimed he was crazy, the authorities wouldn't discharge him because it is normal to claim to be crazy under wartime conditions. On the other hand, if he didn't do anything, he wouldn't be noticed at all. In short, there was no way out. This is Catch-22.

People easily establish similar conditions for themselves. For example, in order for a person to be happy he or she decides that he or she has to have a charming mate, *but* in order to get that mate, he or she would have to look like Robert Redford or Farrah Fawcett-Majors. Since the person doesn't look that good and probably never will (even with plastic surgery), he or she can't be happy. Success appears impossible, and he or she thus makes only token efforts or no effort at all to meet prospective mates.

When the Catch-22 principle is used, the person sometimes views himself as a victim of impossible circumstances or as a loser. While this view frequently brings on gloomy and depressed moods, the excuse makes it easy to give up, to assume the role of a self-declared martyr while feeling good because one is so nobly facing impossible "conditions."

## RECOGNIZING AND DEALING WITH MENTAL DIVERSIONS

It will probably be initially uncomfortable to expose your mental diversions to yourself, but by so doing you'll increase self-understanding, improve skills in self-evaluation, and heighten opportunities for freedom from procrastination.

- Mentally note six activities you are currently putting off, that you suspect you are subconsciously diverting yourself from completing because you've adopted and given credibility to a mental diversion.

- Make up a worksheet on which you identify procrastination activities with mental diversions. You can use the following format:

| Activity | Mental Diversion | Category |
|---|---|---|
| Putting off losing weight | Think it will be easier to start tomorrow | Mañana |
| | Think it will be better to start to lose weight after reading a book on dieting | Contingency mañana |
| | Don't think I have the ability to succeed—ability to persevere is lacking | Catch-22 |
| Failing to return phone calls | Don't know what I will say right now | Mañana |
| | [implication that what to say will be better known tomorrow] | |
| Making an appointment for a medical or dental checkup | Too much of a hassle to call right now | Mañana |
| | Rather wait to see if the problems get worse | Contingency mañana |

- Once patterns have been exposed, try to change the pattern by establishing an objective for each put-off activity. As an example, let's take "I want to weigh 150 pounds and maintain my weight at that level."
- Determine what you will have to do to meet that objective. (Determine the number of daily calories needed to maintain weight at 150 pounds.)
- On average, over each weekly period, do not exceed the daily number of calories required to maintain your weight at 150 pounds.
- Determine how to counter mental diversions by verbalizing aloud to yourself: "What seems tough to start today will probably be just as tough tomorrow." "I certainly can begin the

first step, so I must have the ability to follow with the second step." "Even if I don't have the ability to complete the program before I start, I can learn to develop my skills as I go."

- Recognize that creating a self-loathing outlook because you see yourself having used mental diversions before is just another distraction that turns a real silk purse (recognizing your problem) into a sow's ear.

- Recognize that if you can invent mental diversions, you have creative powers that can be channeled for purposeful ends. See if you can't *imagine* a way to convert mental diversions into creative productivity.

## EMOTIONAL DIVERSIONS

People who think they need to feel good sometimes resort to the use of chemicals: shooting dope to melt the pangs of psychic pain (a state of mental diarrhea) and to produce euphoria; smoking pot or drinking alcohol to get a high, gain insight, or to forget; taking amphetamines to speed up and stimulate; popping Valium to calm and tranquilize; trying vitamin B-15 to energize. To feel good, people also resort to religion (to feel the goodness of a god), grovel for love and admiration of others to get a psychic kick, or get absorbed in ideas (not deeds) of glory for a psychic high. In the end, all such "feel good" methods fail because they don't solve real problems, like finding a way to build the better mousetrap or to communicate warmly.

Another method of feeling good is to get rid of bad feelings (anxiety, depression) by concentrating on forcing the feelings out of awareness. Singing or repeating rhymes to oneself is one way of blocking feelings, and this method sometimes temporarily works. Going on a hunt to find irrational ideas that are causing your feeling bad sometimes serves as a diversion, not a cure. Generally, however, the person attempts to drive away the unwanted feeling as well as the tormenting thoughts that accompany it. This is attempted by trying to will the feeling to go away. But such attempts typically result in deeper envelopment in the unwanted feeling. And it is this focusing hard upon getting rid of the feeling that constitutes an emotional diversion. The person becomes more entangled with unpleasant thoughts about the feeling, desperately ruminates on how to get rid of the feeling, neglecting the real problem.

There are many processes of emotional diversion. One process involves the following sequence: a person first experiences a negative feeling (anxiety), becomes increasingly aware of it, and then decides to get rid of the anxiety to feel good. This desire leads to attempts to force the feeling to go away. But the feeling doesn't disappear. Perhaps the anxiety is an emotional signal that a problem exists that requires attention. Trying to squelch the feeling doesn't get rid of its trigger. Perhaps thinking about the feeling and trying to force it out of awareness only fuels it. In any event, the more effort expended trying to eliminate the feeling, the more the feeling persists.

Sometimes this process starts rapidly. The person fears feeling bad, is sensitive to slight, negative emotional changes, and with a downturn in the emotional barometer escalates the process to panic proportions with a triggering anticipation such as "Oh, no, here it [the feeling of anxiety] comes again!" Now it becomes all the more important to stop the flow of feelings.

Strong concentration on forcing the rapidly escalating anxiety out of awareness, rather than on solving the problems that may have created it, leads to *double troubles* because the actor not only suffers the original anxiety, but now anguishes over the anxiety.

Sometimes, escalating attempts to get free from the feeling of anxiety leads to what I call *emotional drunkenness*. This is where one becomes nearly totally absorbed in fearing the feeling, becomes ensnared into the feeling, and feels overwhelmed, helpless, and impotent.

The flip side of this emotional diversion is becoming enraptured with a positive feeling by getting carried away with good feelings. Upon receiving a compliment, one might glow and preen to a state of ecstatic excitement. Once one is aware of this great glow, efforts are made to sustain it, and this has the opposite effect of trying to squelch a negative feeling—the good feeling proves too slippery to grasp.

Trying to force out the negative and grasp the positive leads to procrastination for obvious reasons. Available energies are directed to seemingly valid but nonproductive ends such as "feeling better." Real problems are put off as pseudo-problems are created, and the affected person comes to think of him- or herself as "out of control."

## DEALING WITH EMOTIONAL DIVERSIONS

Getting engulfed in unpleasant feelings often is a result of seeking answers to the wrong questions. By asking yourself, "How am I going to feel less tense . . . how am I going to feel happy?" you are asking for a magical way to manufacture a good feeling. These "feel good" questions are incomplete at best because they don't address what is needed to be done for *getting it done*. Thus the question is misleading and counterproductive. For example:

John wondered how he was going to feel less tense when he attended a business conference to present facts on a computer program his company had developed. One solution might be to learn Edmond Jacobson's relaxation technique or to pop tranquilizers. Either solution might help reduce tension. But since John was attending the conference to make a presentation, the relevant question was "How can I make my talk effective? What strategies can I employ to make my points clear?" When John asked relevant questions, he healthfully passed over the contingency questions and dealt directly with the problem. As a byproduct of his working to solve the problem, he overcame his tension.

The following steps may help you to accomplish similar goals:

- Review instances in which you become entangled in negative feelings.

- Make a mental note of what you are attempting to accomplish in such circumstances.

- Jot down the external problems that you are trying to contend with and ask questions concerning how you can accomplish such objectives (rather than become absorbed in a hapless pursuit of trying to feel better).

- Sometimes when you begin to feel flooded with anxieties (depressions) it helps to give up the struggle to control the feelings and to simultaneously engage in activity directed at contending with the problem over which you are anxious. So rather than rid yourself of the anxiety directly, try shifting your attention to acting purposefully to resolve the problem.

- If you become enveloped in excitement, it is just as important to frame a question concerning what you are overresponding about. Even though exaggerated feelings of elation are profoundly pleasant while they last, to maintain a state of objectivity, it is just as critical to be realistic about the sources of these excited feelings as it is to be realistic about the negative feelings.

# In and Out of the Quagmire

"Happiness is a by-product of doing something else first."

Mental, action, and emotional diversions are like smokescreens veiling self-doubts and fears of discomfort. These forms of procrastination are but tips of the psychological iceberg, as people who repeatedly fail to resolve their basic psychological problems often become entangled in a bramble bush of false contingencies. I call these false contingencies the *happiness contingencies* because the person adhering to these principles tends to believe that when these contingencies are met, he or she will have a good life. These contingencies result in putting off the doable and involve primarily needs for: control, perfection (success), and approval (a fourth contingency may be a contingency for comfort).

The happiness contingencies are like the contingency mañana. The contingency for control, for example, is based upon the view that one must be in control in order to be happy and productive. To be in control often involves acting perfectly, and with perfectly controlled actions, one can't help but gain approval and feel comfortable.

The odds are that if you make any one of these contingencies a necessity, the others will be subordinate. For example, if you assert that you must be appreciated (approved of, loved, respected), then you will have to act successful in order to get the approval.

With the successful attainment of approval presumably comes a sense of comfort and well-being, and you would probably then judge yourself as being in control. But what if you lose that approval or fail to attain it?

Entanglements in these happiness contingencies result in distraction from awareness of basic problems, and people who routinely procrastinate become involved in these evasions.

The happiness contingencies hold promise for an opportunity to polish one's image. Thus, at one level, it seems to make sense to grapple to gain control, drive for success, or grovel for approval. However, paradoxically, the venture to attain these contingencies proves to be a quixotic undertaking—an "impossible dream." Those who devote their efforts to this venture meet the fate of old Don Quixote when he challenged the windmill.

The illustration on the next page describes this process of striving to achieve the happiness contingencies and the process of envelopment in action, emotional, and mental diversions. As can be seen, the three diversionary systems and the three happiness contingencies can be quite entangling and formidable. They can block purposeful action. Purposeful action, however, is on a completely different pathway, and once the person is on that pathway, the contingencies are circumvented.

Extracting oneself from the quagmire is sometimes difficult

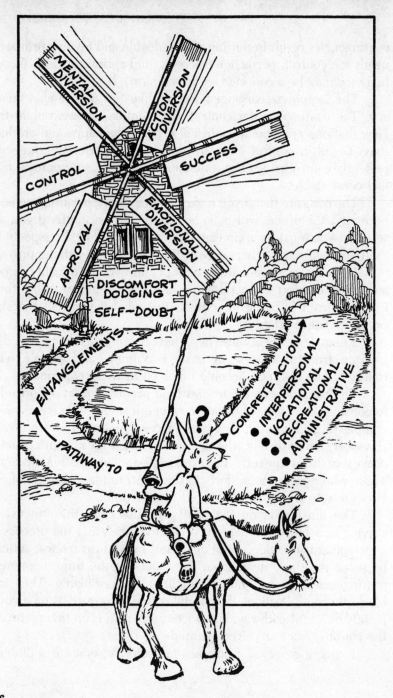

because when one keeps an eye upon meeting the contingencies, one is like a self-spy, watching and evaluating each and every motion, thus promoting more distraction.

This chapter is intentionally quite short. Its purpose has been to identify the three happiness contingencies as snares on the pathway to progress. As David Ausubel suggests, it is important to have a good abstract idea of the concepts you are going to be working with, as it makes it easier to tie the specifics onto that framework. This chapter provides the framework; Chapters 4, 5, and 6 (and to a lesser degree, Chapter 7) provide the specifics.

# Control:
# The Pathway
# to and from
# Procrastination

"Who can control a sunset?"

One warm September morning when I was a young soldier marching with my platoon, I became very much aware of the pathway bordered with green grass stretching like a giant carpet to the awaiting woods. It was the pathway, the sergeant said, on which prisoners of war had marched many years before. I felt their loneliness as I imagined what it must have been like to have walked the path with stoic guards on either side like pickets on a fence segmenting the grass and the woods. I felt a sense of unity that moment and a sense of oneness as a part of the vastness of time.

I have had that sensation at times since: as I've sat on the dry grass watching the brightening glow of yellow warmth moving imperceptibly higher in the morning sky; as I've rested surrounded with dark green leaves and rays of sunshine near the top of a mountain; as I've heard the first rumbling of an engine I had torn apart and rebuilt.

Moments I have also appreciated have been those when I said what I meant—not in harshness or compassion, anger' or fear—in words of simple honesty. When I've tried to control what I've said to reflect what others wanted to hear, I've experienced those moments with a sense of sadness and dejection.

On a country road, at the moment of sunrise, at the birth of an engine, and in the ring of simple truth, I have felt and thought with a clarity of mind and spirit that I can still feel. True, I was in control; I was automatically inhibiting extraneous thoughts; I was restricting my outlook; I was disciplined. But I thought of none of these—I was free, the master of my own experience.

Healthy control, the control of the experience of the country path, is good, useful, and invisible. It is an unconscious process of regulation, a silent coordination of actions, a guidance system that is a tool, not an aim.

When I've tried to be in control, I've spoiled my own experience. I have distanced myself when I have thought about what I was doing, rather than doing what I was thinking. When I've trusted my own values and sense of morality, I've not had to think about maintaining control, and I have rarely created unnecessary troubles for anyone, including myself. But when I haven't trusted myself to trust my values and to do what I thought was right, I have often created needless problems for others and for myself, and I have felt a gnawing sense of frustration and incompleteness grow within.

People I have known who procrastinate have psychological needs for control, and the more effort that goes into establishing that control, the more gets put off and the more compelling and coercive the need for control becomes. Too often the procrastination reflects a choice to eliminate self-doubt and to assure comfort by trying to gain control over one's own thoughts (and feelings and actions), the actions and thoughts and feelings of others, and/or the environment. The first attempt to control goes against reality— mental intrusions are inevitable (sometimes creativity flows from such intrusions); states of pure concentration are rare. It bears emphasis that the harder a person tries to command or force himself to concentrate, the more elusive concentration becomes. Trying to control the thoughts and actions of others is even more difficult. And attempting to control by coercion leads to two unsavory outcomes: restriction at best and revolution at worst.

Complete control over the environment can lead to psychological nirvana. However, after millions of years of trying, we have collectively advanced but have not succeeded in obtaining complete control. The environment can be changed and modified (like people) only up to a certain point. One can't stop it from raining just because the hour has come for picnicking.

The psychological need for control leads to psychological malfunctioning in at least two ways. First, the need creates an impossible condition for gaining self-confidence and comfort. Secondly, this need is really a form of the contingency mañana and has all its drawbacks. The psychological need for control translates into a system in which control is the contingency for self-confidence and comfort. And when the control contingency is the focus, real contingencies (the actual concrete steps in the process of goal attainment) are relegated to the background.

Sometimes focusing upon control is normal, especially when learning a new skill. However, even here the person becomes temporarily distracted from allowing the skill to develop naturally through feedback and practice. Beginning skiers, for example, often report feeling apprehensive and awkward the first few times they look down the slope before launching their descent. When the new skier tries to control each movement, he flounders, falls, and begins again. With practice and developing skill, the skier tends more and more to concentrate upon his or her destination rather than on controlling each separate movement.

Even though concentrating on controlling each motion may be normal, the skier who concentrates on learning skiing—getting down the hill—learns faster than the person concentrating on separate, fragmented movements. This process of not concentrating on separate skills adds to better performance: Exhilaration and accomplishment reward such efforts.

Once a skill is developed, if one uses the mind largely to observe one's own performance, defeat typically follows. Although it is occasionally helpful to monitor your play, if you play tennis and during the game shift concentration away from the game to evaluate how hard you hit the ball, how fit you feel, or the strength of your forearm strokes, you likely will score fewer points. If you dwell upon questions of how the gang will evaluate your play or how you can maintain calm composure, your play will reflect these mental distractions. Continuing to spy on how you are doing rather than playing the game, you may become discouraged and eventually quit.

The difference between trying to meet the contingency of coercive control and meeting the challenge of productive activity where control is invisible is the difference between absorbing oneself in self-doubt and absorbing oneself in the concrete activities of living. Absorption in self-doubt leads to inactivity, but absorption in a concrete activity, such as giving a speech, involves acting. The task is just as simple and straightforward as that. But self-doubt easily fouls up this plan as when a Broadway player anxiously questions himself by asking: "Will I make a smash hit?" (success); "Will people love or hate me for what I have to say?" (approval); "Can I stop feeling tense?" (control). All these questions project contingency thinking in which the actor views playing his or her part from the vantage point of self-image polishing, feeling good, or avoiding failure.

Control, for many procrastinators, is a prerequisite for achieving success and gaining approval, which in turn are contingencies for wiping out self-doubts and attaining a state of comfort. Typically, a person obsessed with how to gain control gives momentum to self-doubt and makes discomfort more feared than before. Indeed, panic may follow such obsessive preoccupations as the anxiety brewing out of these obsessions blocks further progress.

Failing to meet the contingency of control, the person may turn defeat into victory: Not having control can provide a soothing but false explanation for unhappiness—"I'm not in control, so I can't possibly succeed." This explanation, though false, can be comforting.

Naturally, the above contingencies are ordered backward. A forward pathway is to work to accomplish the daily tasks that are the contingencies for efficiency and effectiveness. Building confidence and tolerance for discomfort also requires following forward pathways.

## GAINING CONTROL WITHOUT REALLY TRYING

The following exercises may, at first glance, appear to have little directly to do with getting it done. Their purpose is to help you increase your flexibility, and increased flexibility is strongly related to increased ability to do it now.

- Sometimes control is attempted through acquiring knowledge. But the would-be controller often gathers the materials of knowledge like books, magazines, and newspapers, but doesn't do the work of reading, perhaps in recognition that this plan, designed exclusively to use knowledge to gain control, won't work. So if you have accumulated learning materials over the years and have not used them, consider abandoning them except for the one or two you deem most important. Abandon them by throwing them out or giving them away. Don't store them. Let go of the collection, then concentrate on the one or two selected projects. Such action can start you working from a clean slate.

- Place yourself in a situation in which it is necessary for you to have trust in someone—a situation in which you will have to depend upon that person for a moment for your physical well-being. A popular exercise is to ask a friend or family member to catch you as you fall backward. To do this, position yourself such that you are standing upright with ample room to fall backward. Your partner positions himself behind you, then signals you to fall backward, and you do so like a stiff board while your partner catches you in mid-descent. Naturally, if you weigh 500 pounds don't expect a midget to support your weight. Exercise your judgment in the selection of a partner in this exercise. Repeat this exercise as many times as required for you to feel relaxed as you fall backward. (This exercise is also used for building trust.)

- Turn your world around by doing an exercise in differences. If you are a shabby dresser, dress sharply for a day. If you are a sharp dresser, dress shabbily for a day. If you normally drive to work but can use public transportation, take the public transportation for a day or a week. If you avoid saying "Hello" to people where you work or go to school, say, "Hello." If you normally say, "Hello," say, "Hi." If you have relative freedom of choice as to how to structure your work day, take some tasks you normally reserve for doing at the end of the afternoon and do them first thing in the morning. If you exercise in the morning, exercise in the evening instead. Have your supper in the morning and breakfast in the evening. If you want to give up smoking and are inclined to be introverted, shout out, "Addicted!" each time you light up a cigarette.

These exercises are only a sample of the strategies that can be used to increase your flexibility and make it easier for you to adapt to more varied situations.

Control difficulties sometimes go undetected but can be identified if you know where to look. You can use the following criteria to identify areas in which you may have a control problem. Symptoms of a control problem include (but are not limited to):

- talking very softly
- talking very loudly
- agreeing with a "yes," then adding the word "but" ("Yes, you're probably right, but . . .")
- not hearing what people say
- not being aware of the many elements that constitute your environment (like one of my clients, who after six sessions noticed that the window in the office was adorned with plants only when it was pointed out)
- working frantically
- resisting new ideas
- repeating the same daily routine slavishly
- making demands
- consistently trying to get the last word in
- bodily stiffness
- a sense of obsessive urgency (confusion about what to do first coupled with an urgency to complete everything)
- hostile feelings
- a sense of impotence
- talking too fast
- being silent in a group

If you note that any of these examples apply to you, then try the appropriate exercise(s) among the following:

- Speak half as rapidly.
- Speak up in the groups in which you normally remain quiet.
- Make yourself heard.
- Tone down your voice.
- Let people have their say without defending yourself.
- Summarize and feed back to others what they have said to you.

- Discover one new thing each day about your extended environment; do this every day for the rest of your life.
- Work "planfully" rather than frantically.
- Experiment with potentially helpful activities you feel resistant to doing.
- Change one element in your routine each day, then go back to the old way if you don't find it satisfying.
- Instead of making one demand, have five alternate solutions available.
- Relax by concentrating your attention on your belly button; do this for five minutes every day.
- Among your many incomplete tasks, pick one at random and do it (use a paper bag and deposit task titles and select one by drawing).
- Find three positive ways to view each hostility-provoking situation.
- Identify one strength per day; do this exercise for one year.
- Learn a new game or sport in which you have to rely on others to help you learn; or if you generally rely on others, learn a game or sport in which you instruct yourself.
- Practice operating from concepts. Instead of worrying about the words that you use to express yourself, try to be clear on the concept you want to express (friendliness, dissatisfaction) and let the words flow from the concept.
- Visit a tranquil place and allow your eyes, hearing, sense of smell, touch, and mind to wander.

# Perfectionism: Fear of Failure

"Every garden has its weeds."

Daedalus, the builder of the Cretan labyrinth, had overstepped his bounds. He had placed wings on the arms of his son, Icarus, and given him the gift of flight. This act so angered Zeus, the father of the gods, that when Icarus ascended in the sky, Zeus caused the sun to melt the wax that bound the feathers to Icarus's flesh. Icarus fell into the sea, and Zeus made him into the island of Icaria.

This Greek myth inspired Henry Murray to call compulsive

striving for perfection the *Icarus complex*. Murray saw that people have a drive to master their environment—a perfectly normal and quite desirable drive. He also saw that people could escalate the normal drive and become entangled in a pursuit for success or perfection, and when they did so, Murray thought, the fate of Icarus lay before them.

Murray is in good company in observing the effects of forsaking all for perfection. Alfred Adler also insightfully noted that many people extend the normal drive for success by translating this quest into a *need* to heroically transcend themselves. Such attempts he saw as plainly vain, and vanity he saw as neurotic. Karen Horney, Adler's contemporary, posited that neurosis is a state of imagining and then trying to live up to an idealized and glorified self-image. Albert Ellis has recently defined this state as a dire need "to be thoroughly competent, intelligent, and achieving in all possible aspects." So what begins as a normal desire or drive to achieve success becomes coverted psychologically into a requirement. The person *requiring* success is one who is preoccupied with the pursuit of attaining the impossible dream of perfection.

The psychological need for success is a joy-dissipating mental monster stemming from the false belief that perfection is achievable. Everyday observations repeatedly illustrate that there are limits to perfectability and that all humans are fallible. People who deny this reality and strain to contradict it tend to hold in common a remarkably similar set of rules.

Horney has pointed out that when a person demands perfection of himself, he condemns himself to obeying a rigid set of rules for achieving this idealized state. Both Horney and Ellis point out that these rules are cast in the form of *shoulds*, *oughts*, and *musts*.\* For example, if you believe that you *must* be perfect and then don't

---

\*Not all *should*, *ought*, and *must* statements are absolutist. Some are conditional. For example, when I say, "I should go to the grocery store," I am not necessarily imposing a demand upon myself. Instead, the phrase serves as a reminder. The absolutist *should* (demand), on the other hand, is disruptive rather than instructive, because such a command results in oppositionalism, performance anxieties, anger, and other distracting psychological states.

perform well enough, you are apt to chastise and deprecate your-self for failing. In addition, as you continue to perform less than perfectly, you may become cynical and defeatist and begin to characterize yourself as a total failure.

Linked to this unrealistic striving for perfection is a fear of failure. People fear failing because of the painful feelings of anxiety and depression they typically experience when their perfectionistic ideals are not attained. But instead of working to change their outlook to conform to reality, they desperately cling to their belief in perfectionism and manage to temporarily avoid the bad feelings attached to failure (doing something imperfectly) by procrastinat-ing.

Fear of failure and procrastination can grow to enormous proportion. By setting absolute standards and rules to be followed perfectly, you are apt to dodge working hard at what you think will be unsuccessful, or you may work with a sense of obsessive urgency where you worry while you work and at the same time perceive yourself falling further and further behind.

Another clever tactic that stems from a fear of failure and that covers over anxious/depressed feelings is waiting until the eleventh hour (the proverbial last minute) to begin something that portends possible imperfection. Now the imperfect work can be ex plained—"I started too late; next time I'll do it right!" Despite the self-con, a dim awareness exists that the time was available to do a better job, but that the time was mismanaged. Even so, the con (developed through that double-edged sword, the intellect) helps maintain a false sense of well-being.

When success is conceived of as a solution for resolving inner doubts, chances are that if you procrastinate, some of your procras-tinating can be linked to a fear of failing. The person who believes in this contingency solution believes that success is essential for creating a sense of self-worth and for making life meaningful. Not only is this belief erroneous, but it abets a type of self-focused concern that drains available energies. And the procrastination that results from this self-preoccupation increases chances for more failure.

When success is the prerequisite for resolving inner doubts and for making life meaningful, we once again face a contingency problem similar to the control contingency problem. Here again, a condition is established that seems on the surface to be reasonable—be perfect and your problems will evaporate. Noble though striving for perfection may sound, it is still the equivalent of trying to inspire yourself to paddle upstream when where you want to go is downstream.

## ANTIPERFECTIONISM EXERCISES

Awareness-of-human-limitations exercises help build tolerance for mistake making. After completing these exercises, use what you have learned by undertaking a problem you've been ducking because you've feared failure.

- Carry out a dialogue with yourself on the topic of how people grow and learn through both mistakes and successes.
- Pretend you're a research scientist assigned the task of understanding and explaining why people can't be perfect. Write a one-page report summarizing your findings.
- Pretend you are an investigative reporter assigned to write an article on what constitutes success and fulfillment to you. Outline the article.
- List normally occurring impediments that could slow you down from doing the best you can at any one time.

It is helpful to ask yourself if you hold some negative and faulty assumptions about yourself that hook you into a need for success to prove your worth. If so, rather than anticipate failure and lament over not succeeding, try to get an alternate perspective on your need-for-success problem by answering the following questions:

- If I'm not the person I "should" be, what's wrong with my being the person I am?
- What ten things do I appreciate most about myself?
- What can I tell myself that is compassionate if I don't perform as well as I would like?
- Success gives me an advantage, but how does success make me a noble person?
- What makes less-than-perfect performance so unacceptable to me?

Risk taking and opportunity creating are helpful to people who try to cover up their faults. To break free from perfectionism, it is important to break down the conceited view that you *must* maintain a flawless appearance.

- Purposefully make some of your work less "perfect" than usual.
- Try undertaking a difficult project that you've hithertofore wanted to start but haven't because your initial performance would have been poor.
- Admit some of your errors to a close friend.
- Compassionately support someone who seems frustrated with his poor work performance.

Sensory-appreciation exercises are helpful for persons who focus on success to the exclusion of their sensory experiences. Becoming aware and appreciative of information from your sensory experiences provides a tranquil, refreshing experiential interlude that can help you to feel like getting it done now.

- Take a walk each day and be visually alert to new discoveries.
- Stop for five minutes each day to become aware of the varied sounds in your environment.
- Touch a new object each day. Close your eyes and concen-

trate upon the texture and form of the object. Learn as much as you can about the object from touch alone.

- Find something new and pleasant to smell each day.

Select an activity you are putting off because you are afraid you will not perform well enough and follow through completing it. While you are involved in the activity, use the experience for self-improvement. The following six-step method can be used to achieve the goal of self-improvement using the activity of your choice:

- Identify one trouble area (usually this is a situation in which you are uncomfortable or anxious).
- Appraise your performance capability and establish what you think are realistic goals (not perfection).
- Establish subgoals so as to define steps for accomplishing each goal.
- Develop strategies for accomplishing the goal(s).
- Carry out the strategies for accomplishing the goal(s).
- Revise strategies as conditions warrant.

## A NEED FOR CERTAINTY

There is a story of a gerbil, weak from hunger, that chanced upon two heads of cabbage. Confused as to which was the better, he pondered the decision until he starved.

Some people who routinely procrastinate act like the gerbil. Faced with making a decision, they feel distressed over the possibility of not making the right choice and wait for a guarantee that the decision will result in success (the "perfect" choice). While anxiously awaiting the guarantee, they put off trying to get the facts that might make for a more enlightened decision.

At least part of the indecision generates from the belief that one has to be sure before acting. Part of the indecisiveness reflects an avoidance of possible self-criticism that might result from making an error. Both views would hardly ever have been subscribed to by General George Patton. Indeed, he believed that if you have a plan you are 80 percent sure of, "violently execute it." I would go one step further. If you are faced with a difficult decision, such as choosing between Harvard and Yale, a Ford or a Chevrolet, after you've done a reasonable amount of research, all you need be is 50.5 percent sure in order to make your decision. Fifty-and-one-half percent certainty is as good a reason for choosing a Ford over a Chevrolet as 51 percent is. If your decision is that you view your alternatives as equally desirable, then flip a coin.

Although there is no sure formula that guarantees the correctness of the decision before the results are in, inaction due to indecisiveness is the wrong decision in the vast majority of instances. Indeed, it is this very point that prompted the proverb "He who hesitates is lost."

Indecisiveness has thus far been highlighted as a problem. The reality is, however, that most people make decisions relatively easily most of the time. If you are about to run short of food, you unhesitatingly go to the grocery store. If you want to go to the seashore, you decide when you will leave and what form of transportation you will take. It is doubtful that you will criticize yourself for choosing to buy your groceries from the A&P or for leaving for the shore at 8:00 instead of 8:15 A.M.

We feel comfortable about many decisions, like shopping for food, because we can predict the outcome. Practically everyone can and does make many such decisions daily, and in most instances the decisions are rendered fairly automatically. What complicates this decision-making process is the interjection of self-doubts and self-criticism.

Faced with an either/or decision, such as purchasing a Chevrolet or a Ford, a person can make himself sick over the thought of making a "wrong" decision. This indecisiveness can accelerate to a state where the person does nothing, becomes more dissatisfied, and worries about every imaginable problem that can result from a "wrong" decision.

This perfectionist demand to make a failure-proof decision distorts perception and impedes progress. Thus indecisiveness represents a breakdown in the decision-making sequence. The following illustrates the breakdown process in contrast to an effective decision-making process.

## THE DECISION-MAKING PROCESS

Using the following decision-making model, apply it to a problem area in which you have been and continue to be indecisive. Test the decision-making model against this problem. (For contrast, a breakdown in the decision process is also illustrated to alert you to the steps in the process you will want to avoid.)

### TWO DIRECTIONS TO CHOOSE

| Decision-Making Process | Breakdown in Decision-Making Process |
|---|---|
| 1. Clear statement of issues | Vague and confusing conceptualization of the issues |
| 2. Objective statement of current position in relation to the issues | Loss of sense of orientation |
| 3. Assessment of similarities and differences among the alternatives | Envelopment in feelings of self-doubt, self-downing, shame, and/or helplessness |
| 4. Deciding on steps to reduce uncertainty | Escalating indecisiveness and inhibition through double troubles |
| 5. Testing steps through taking action | Taking steps to divert from tension |
| 6. Making decision based upon the outcome of previous decisions | Repetition of the same problem |

The following is a concrete example of how you can apply the decision-making process to the selection of an automobile. Under the heading "Assessment of Similarities and Differences," the question marks represent gaps in your knowledge that you will try to fill in. The section "Deciding on Steps to Reduce Uncertainty" describes this process.

## 1. Statement of Issues

Repair old automobile or purchase new automobile (probably a Ford or a Chevrolet).

## 2. Statement of Position

Old auto currently averaging $60 per month in repairs. Tires now need replacing. Reliable auto necessary as job involves some use of auto, and income is lost when auto is inoperative. Situation requires quick action.

## 3. Assessment of Similarities and Differences

| Factors | Keep Old Car | Buy Ford | Buy Chevy |
|---|---|---|---|
| Estimated yearly repair and part replacement costs | $750 | Minimal | Minimal |
| Estimated depreciation for a year's use | $250 | ? | ? |
| Automobile frequency-of-repair ratings (Consumer Reports) | Fair | ? | ? |
| Under warranty, does the dealer provide a replacement automobile during repairs? | Not applicable | ? | ? |
| Dealer reputation (estimates) | Not applicable | ? | ? |

| | 17 mpg | 24 mpg | 27 mpg |
|---|---|---|---|
| Gasoline mileage (estimates) | | | |
| Styling | Like | Like | Like |
| Purchase price | Not applicable | ? | ? |
| Sales tax | Not applicable | ? | ? |

## 4. Deciding on Steps to Reduce Uncertainty

Obtain data on depreciation of Ford and Chevrolet. Check *Consumer Reports* on frequency-of-repair ratings. Check prospective dealer to see if replacement car is provided if new automobile breaks down and requires extensive repairs. Check sales tax and purchase prices of new automobiles.

## 5. Testing Steps Through Taking Action

This is the process of gathering missing data.

## 6. Making Decision

Purchase Ford from dealer—because:

- fair deal
- free replacement automobile (Chevrolet dealer does not provide)
- lower probability of breakdown

Although this decision-making process requires work, the model can be designed to provide the relevant data necessary to make most decisions; and the systematic use of this model subverts the decision-making-breakdown process. Furthermore, in using this model, you are continuously in action; even when you are not decided on the final outcome, you are taking a logical pathway toward making that decision. Also, since no two options are identical, there will be "tradeoffs." For example, you give up one feature you like in the Chevrolet to get the Ford with a different feature.

Arnold Lazarus indicates that anxiety and indecisiveness arise in part because you may feel helpless to cope with future problems the decision may create. You might purchase the Ford, for example, only to watch the dealer go out of business; or you could buy a lemon; or Chevrolet may have a sale; and so on. Lazarus's solution to these "what if . . .?" type problems is to add one word to the "what if . . .?" sequence: "so what if . . .?" By thinking in "so what if . . .?" terms, you will find the potential problems not so oppressive.

## VINDICTIVE PERFECTIONISM

The God of the Old Testament, Jehovah, punished those who disobeyed and offended him. Adam and Eve were evicted from paradise for eating the apple of knowledge of good and evil. Because of his disobedience, Jonah was forced to live in the stomach of a whale for three days. Noah's ark saved two of every species from drowning when Jehovah flooded the earth to destroy all other life in retaliation against those humans who disobeyed his laws.

Jehovah had an anger problem. He set down laws, expected people to follow them, and became wrathful and destructive when they failed to comply.

Jehovah's attitude exemplifies the destructive urges within all people. These destructive urges often follow a predictable pattern. First there is an expectation that rules or laws must be obeyed (perfectionism). Secondly, there is a myopic view that others operate by inferior rules and laws and therefore must be forced, if necessary, to acquiesce to the "right rules." Third, if these others are suspected to know the "right rules" and disobey, or fail to heed a warning, the urge is to punish them.

Sometimes this process reflects willful self-indulgence. An employer who asserts his authority by shouting at employees whenever he pleases and a parent who screams at a child because the child does not behave according to the parent's rules are both • behaving in a Jehovah-like manner.

If, on the other hand, an adversary is perceived as too powerful, the outward expression of anger and the urge to punish may be squelched and turned inward. Suppose, for example, you work for the above-mentioned boss and have been unable to secure another position because of poor job opportunities in your region. You currently need the money you earn for rent and food. You correctly believe that your boss is wrong for acting so consistently with anger but are helpless to change his attitude and behavior. You feel legitimately helpless but add to your woes by labeling yourself as weak, ineffectual, and no good. You expect yourself to be stronger than this tyrant, and that is why you punish yourself. You are your own Jehovah in action against yourself, and no one needs to explain to you how rotten that feels.

Sometimes one may be in a position of power like Jehovah's and feel good while feeling angry. One day I was discussing the concept of anger with a group of psychotherapy trainees. In examining the effects of anger, one trainee proudly reported that his anger felt good. The example he gave involved an incident in which he went to retrieve his clothing from the dry cleaner and noticed a tiny spot on his coat. In vivid detail he told how he had yelled and screamed at and cursed the shopkeeper for the damage. He exclaimed how he had frightened this person, humbled him, and forced him to remove the spot immediately.

The trainee believed that yelling was the way to show power. He had learned this technique from an encounter group experience. He further believed that because he was on the customer's side of the counter, he had the unique right to be a glorious Jehovah. Like the judge in a kangaroo court, he indicted, tried, condemned, and punished the shopkeeper, and believed he showed his power and strength in doing so.

In anger, violators of the unwritten law are rapidly identified and condemned. As in Dante's *Inferno*, they are to suffer the perils of hell or purgatory. However, most of the time angry impulses are not acted out directly because of the potentially disastrous social consequences. Thus anger is likely to be internalized and repeated in the form of obsessive reruns of the evocative situation. The person who believes his boss is a tyrant may, in addition to fuming over his perceived weakness, entertain fantasies about being powerful enough to force the boss to be subservient or even powerful enough to actually annihilate the boss.

Anger can develop out of a feeling of helplessness (first cousin to self-doubt) and/or intolerance of tension and discomfort. When anger develops from helplessness, the first reaction is fear. But since fear clashes with the ideal image, the fear or feeling of helplessness is blunted and a pseudo-anger erupts. In other words, the person defuses the fear by acting angry and "sounding tough." And this person becomes self-deluded in believing the reaction is a healthy anger. The reaction is comparable to the puffing up of a blow-fish who perceives danger. With people, this defensive scenario only serves to blunt objective evaluation of the situation.

Intolerance of tension occurs when a rule or desire is thwarted and the person believes that he *should not* have to bear inconvenience or frustration. Such frustration, stemming from being thwarted, is felt to be intolerable. As part of this process, the offending party is devalued, dehumanized, and made punishable for having done something unthinkable—violating the experiencer's expectations. However, instead of a direct outburst, sometimes the expression of this feeling will leak out through oppositionalism, pouting, stubbornness, passive obstructionalism, rebelliousness—and procrastination.

Chronic anger (hostility) generating out of intolerance of tension or helplessness can lead to revenge against an adversary that results in self-harm. Retaliation by the adversary is one obvious outcome. There are other subtle outcomes that reflect self-harm. A hostile adolescent, for example, can get back at the parents by failing in areas the parents can't control. Thus the rebellious adolescent can fail school subjects, date people the parents disapprove of, become overly thin or fat, and be chronically late—much to the parents' chagrin. Although this behavior is equivalent to breaking one's toys so that no one else can play, the rebellious person is often too enveloped in playing Jehovah and seeking revenge to consciously recognize the personal damage such rebellious actions create.

In general, anger and hostility reflect perfectionistic attitudes. Furthermore, anger (hostility), an exercise in futility, impedes life's progress in at least seven ways:

- Enjoyment of living is curtailed because of continual brooding or vengeful scheming.
- Energies are expended blaming and condemning rather than in constructing.
- A high inner-tension level is maintained.
- Distrust becomes increasingly evident toward those who genuinely want to help.
- Retaliation is invited.
- Life tends to be unpleasant.
- Hostile preoccupations distract from purposefulness and thus lead to procrastination.

Obviously, time expended in angry or hostile pursuits drains time from other activities. However, the person engulfed in vengeful thoughts and vengeful actions is oblivious to how valuable time is diverted from the constructive challenges of life.

Anger (hostility) is a manifestation of a maladaptive, primitive style of coping. So let's see what can be done to begin to build up some "emotional muscle" to contend with this *vengeful perfectionism*.

## DEALING WITH HOSTILITY

The following hints to reduce anger obviously cannot result in the complete elimination of this problem and all the procrastination associated with it. However, your awareness of the problem and these "attack" strategies will help get you out of the kangaroo court.

- When you feel hostile, discern whether the feeling comes out of helplessness or intolerance of tension. If the feeling represents helplessness (fear), identify what you're afraid of. Then simulate a set of conditions under which you can practice learning to act in nonhelpless and nonhostile ways. If the feeling represents intolerance for tension, explore what makes tension so intolerable to you.

- Identify situations in which you are likely to become hostile because of low tension tolerance, then imagine yourself in that situation responding in three constructive ways. Validate the three constructive alternatives by role-playing with an objective and kind friend.

- Role-play with a friend three alternative ways of stopping procrastinating in a situation in which you are procrastinating because you wish to punish somebody.

- Use the alternative that seems to be most effective in overcoming procrastination.

- Try to think of five positive qualities of each of your adversaries. When you encounter an adversary, keep these qualities in mind as you interact.

- Try to accept the reality that people are not born to abide by your rules, particularly if you don't tell them what the rules are. Indeed, people have their own rules, and some of these rules are most surely going to conflict with yours.

- Expectations lead to exasperations. So if you feel hostile, look to see what expectations you are holding. Then seek a tolerable alternative view of the situation.

## GUILT TRIP THROUGH THE MIND TUNNEL

On his annual spring cave-hunting expedition in the Adirondack Mountains, Jack wandered far from the trail and chanced to notice a small, deep cave partially covered with scraggy shrubs. With rising anticipation he grasped his flashlight and entered. As he entered, his excitement evaporated. Suddenly the chill of apprehension hit him as memories of the past began to fill his mind. There was Miss Maultsby telling him he was a dirty and bad boy for lifting Susie's dress. He remembered how horrified his mother seemed when Miss Maultsby conveyed the bad news. "I feel like I will die," she said; "you've disgraced the family. We can never live this down." In rapid succession a barrage of images flashed before his mind's eye: how bad Aunt Tilly felt when he forgot to thank her for the handkerchiefs she had given him for his tenth birthday; his father's hurt when he failed math in high school; his first girlfriend, who told him he had "ruined her" and because of that he could never leave her; George, his first boss, who told Jack that he had let him down and that he didn't deserve the break he (Jack) had gotten.

The farther into the tunnel Jack went, the more vivid the guilts and the more quickly they came. Unfortunately, we'll temporarily have to leave Jack in the midst of his plight and take an academic look at guilt.

*Guilt* implies the violation of a moral standard followed by self-condemnation. Guilt is a vindictive perfectionism that takes the form "You *should* have behaved better. Now you're really no good—a real louse."

Although guilt is typically a useless, backward look, sometimes it is an anticipatory reaction leading to procrastination. This is when a person gets caught in a moral *double bind* by trapping himself between two moral opposites. For instance, suppose you believe it is wrong to compete and at the same time value the type of success that comes from effectively competing. This presents quite a dilemma: If you compete, you'll feel guilty for competing, and if you don't compete, you'll feel guilty because you haven't obtained the prize of the competition. Catch-22 strikes again!

Although there are many things to feel guilty over, procrastination need not be included on the list. In my view, if you must procrastinate, pointing the guilty finger at yourself will hardly serve to correct your behavior. Feel remorseful or feel regretful (feeling bad without self-condemnation). Figure out what can be done to unchain your potential. Experience all this, and you are not only moving away from guilt but drifting from procrastination as well.

Well, we left Jack several paragraphs ago suffering by going backward in the mind tunnel. Fortunately, he catches some pages flying by him with the heading "Getting Out of the Mind Tunnel." "What a strange title," Jack contemplates. "I think I'll read it."

## GETTING OUT OF THE MIND TUNNEL

- Ask yourself what makes you a reprehensible person if you fail to live up to a moral standard.
- What double-bind situations are you aware of where you feel guilty?
- Try to collect concrete facts to help you ascertain the validity or nonvalidity of both elements of the double bind.
- Try to see if both sides of the double bind can coexist without your procrastinating or feeling guilty. Alternatively, commit yourself to one direction or the other.
- Give yourself five good reasons why you're not a terrible person even if you do procrastinate.
- Accept responsibility for intentional or unintentional poor acts (like spreading false rumors or withholding affection) and try to spend more energy on preventing their recurrence than on backward looks through the mind tunnel.

# 6

# Approval Seeking and Putting It Off

"Present yourself as a maple and you'll get sapped."

A concept apropos of this chapter is that you are better off trying to please yourself because you can't please everyone.

Since different people have different tastes, it is impossible to please everyone. Furthermore, if you try, chances are that not only will certain others not appreciate the gesture, but you might at the same time displease yourself by failing in this noble venture and by not acting in your own best interest.

Some people, however, are devoted to the idea that the way

to be pleasing to oneself is to please other people. But trying to gain the universal approval and acceptance of others can be a very bad trip—one that has all sorts of noxious consequences, including procrastination. This chapter will explain what approval seeking is, its pitfalls, and how to get rid of it. Shyness, a close cousin to approval seeking, will be treated similarly.

## WHO SEEKS APPROVAL?

Approval seeking is like the contingencies of seeking control and seeking perfection, as the approval seeker believes that gaining approval will provide all the success and happiness that he desires. Like the other contingencies for happiness, approval seeking often has a paradoxical effect, as the following approval-seeking-type problems suggest.

Getting high on the admiration of others results in the emotional drunkenness that I call *love lushism* (another name for approval seeking). When approval seems like an overpowering *need*, failing to obtain it causes painful psychological withdrawal symptoms.

Just as different people vary in their drinking habits, love lushism is a matter of degree. People have varied desires for gaining approval and thus will react differently depending upon the situation at hand. In some situations, love lushism will appear in full force as the person concentrates on obtaining approval at any cost, while that same person can be observed in another situation in which approval is the furthest thing from his mind.

Whatever the provocative situation, when a strong *need* for approval is perceived, the needy person becomes a pawn of his or her urgency. Consider, for example, making a good impression. When one becomes so absorbed in making a good impression that it becomes an urgent drive, one is unfortunately likely to get so entangled in his or her own mental machinations that just the opposite is achieved. Certainly when the majority of a person's energies and powers of concentration are being channeled into an ongoing self-debate ("Should I say or do this or that? What will he/she/they think? I wonder if he/she/they like me, think I'm attractive, smart, witty, . . ." etc.), it is difficult to devote much of oneself to a conversation or activity "out there."

In some instances these internal debates (which arise with the urgent need to gain approval) will result in *confrontation anxieties*—fearing to express an unpopular opinion or idea that might invite a counterpoint or disagreement. Such confrontation anxieties can leave the person looking like a wishy-washy wimp with few opinions or ideas. Another negative outcome of these mental machinations can be a *compliance compulsion*, in which the person decides that gaining the acceptance of those whose approval he seeks so zealously is best accomplished by acquiescing to the others' demands. Unfortunately, being overly compliant typically results in being taken for a patsy, someone who can be walked all over, rather than a person deserving admiration and respect.

Studies of pressures for conformity, including experiments by Stanley Milgram on obedience and compliance, illustrate that most people will comply with group pressures and the directives of those perceived to be in authority. Uniforms and titles like Doctor, Sir, Squire, and Mistress are projected to symbolize authority and make it easy for the approval-seeking member of society to know toward whom they should act particularly deferential and whose word they should unthinkingly accept. Thoughtless compliance is an indicator of how low one places oneself in the societal pecking order.

Contrary to popular beliefs that the meek will inherit the earth, there certainly is no hard evidence that this is likely to take place in the near future. Furthermore, there is no evidence that meekness leading to suffering results in success.

Approval seekers have alternatives to acting meek and passive. One alternative is being the "good guy" (or gal) who acts very friendly and eagerly grants favors at each convenient opportunity. Such an approval-seeking person will habitually consent to do favors for others, even though he or she realizes that the time taken to do the favors robs time from personal pursuits. However, this "good" approval-seeking person often puts off doing the favor as well as personal pursuits and paradoxically gets just the opposite of what he (or she) obstensibly sought—criticism for delaying.

Sometimes anticipating criticism, the approval-seeking person becomes resentful toward others who may be actually doing little or nothing in the way of applying pressure to get the favor done. This group of "good," favor-granting approval seekers stewing with contained resentment are avid putter-offers. Resentment and hostility are prime reasons why many such love lushes procrastinate—to get revenge by acting oppositional and by delaying.

Some people seem to think they need the company of the person who plays the "good guy" role. Because they were brought up to believe they are special princes and princesses, such persons tend to view themselves as a sort of royalty deserving of praise. Since most self-confident persons tend to abstain from lavishing them with praise and adoration, they therefore try to attract the attention of and develop a cadre of people who readily fall into the role of devoted love lushes to lavish them with praise. Such a cadre of "good people" characters tend eventually to create trouble in the royal court with their resentments. And when the "good person" finally turns about, the tables temporarily become reversed. The royal prince or princess affirms the belief that the "good person" is needed, and will apply coercion, if necessary, to maintain the status quo. This royal family gains psychological strength from the seemingly weak, mouselike "good person," and the withdrawal of that dependency prompts a sense of threat. But soon, all is "well" again as the mice and royalty, having similar needs, rejoin to maintain the symbiotic relationship bound by mutual need.

In addition to the futility of self-debating and other negative aspects of love lushism, approval seeking leads to all sorts of procrastination because when caught in the quest for approval, all else becomes secondary, even trivial, in comparison.

Obviously, people who seek approval procrastinate on healthy self-expression. If you think you may have approval-seeking tendencies, don't despair. Fortunately, this psychological hang-up can be corrected. The following are a few suggestions for starting this corrective process.

## DEALING WITH APPROVAL PROBLEMS

There are many ways to deal with approval-seeking problems. One approach is teaching yourself to become desensitized to potential disapproval. By learning to become less sensitive to disapproval you simultaneously become more sensitive to others because your energies are not going into mental machinations, or self-spying— watching and judging each and every one of your social motions. However, becoming more yourself and less needful of approval may require temporary, but sometimes radical and uncomfortable, actions. Here are some suggestions if you are afraid of appearing conspicuous and you want to start to stop worrying about what others think.

- Go to the local diner for breakfast. Ask for the unconventional one fried egg and one scrambled egg instead of two eggs the same style. You're bound to attract attention with this one! You may even find the exercise fun.
- Wear two different-colored shoes for a day.
- Wear your hair in an unusual fashion for a week.
- Wear a turkey feather in your hair for an afternoon.
- Whistle "Dixie" as you walk down the street.
- Step out of character in constructive style. If you normally dress sloppily, dress sharply. If you normally frown, smile. If you don't compliment people, do so. If you are patronizing, be factual. In other words, try to change some of the external things that you do. As a result, you might find people responding more positively toward you.
- Make plans to go out in public with a person you know who tends to act silly. Use the experience to act silly yourself.

- Ask for change in a busy store in which there is a sign reading "No change given." Ask the proprietor to justify his rule. You don't have to be hostile or aggressive, just matter-of-fact.
- If you are dissatisfied with a product, return it. Make a mental note of how well you handled the complaint, and if dissatisfied with your approach, modify it based upon the experience and try out your new approach.

Although you may feel uncomfortable attempting these exercises, that's not uncommon. Furthermore, there is nothing wrong with experiencing discomfort under the above conditions. Indeed, bearing discomfort helps you to build up emotional muscle for discomfort. If you feel embarrassed, however, you are putting yourself down or believing you are exposing a weakness. Now ask yourself: "What weakness am I exposing?" and "What's wrong with temporarily exercising my right to be less conventional than normal?" Well, what *is* wrong with that?

The following exercises extend the concept of overcoming fears of disapproval to areas of self-expression—saying what you mean, standing up for your rights, saying no, expressing opinions, giving feedback, and stepping out of the limelight.

- Have a dialogue with yourself on saying what you mean and meaning what you say. Tape-record this conversation. Play it back and note what you consider to be constructive ideas. Implement one of these ideas each day.
- If you feel you are being pushed around too much, practice, as a preliminary step, standing up for yourself with some of your friends who are willing to help you role-play some new ways of responding. Next, try it on new acquaintances. Remember, others are not going to remain passive as you develop skill in being more self-expressive. However, if you speak from the heart, as the old saying goes, you'll be acting in truth with yourself. Also, the feedback coming out of your interactions may prove that your opinions and ideas aren't 100 percent right in all circumstances. That's fine because that's how you

learn. It's also fine because you will quickly discover that you *can* express yourself.

- If you think the word *no* is naughty, get some practice saying the word. Go to a store where there are pushy sales personnel. Resist their sales pitches by using the word *no*.

- Examine what's wrong with saying no or maybe. What is so great in saying yes when you don't mean yes?

- Formulate an opinion about a controversial news topic and present it to friends or colleagues for their reactions. If a debate ensues, stick to your point. Try to repeat this exercise at least once a week.

- If you feel dissatisfied with someone's behavior, consider if it would be helpful to point this out to him, and if so, put on your diplomat's hat and try.

- If you act like a clown to grab attention, reverse your typical modus operandi and try to make others the favorable center of attention. People like to be thought of as having good ideas or gaining recognition for their good qualities. So you may be able to generate good positive attention for yourself through this exercise without grabbing the limelight for yourself.

## SHYNESS: ANOTHER NAME FOR INTERPERSONAL PROCRASTINATION

As I define it, *shyness* (a special approval-seeking problem) is a fear of making contacts with other people, resulting in avoidance or procrastination on such activities.

Shyness, a special form of procrastination, can be symptomatic of an annoying tendency to dodge interpersonal contacts. However, it can be overcome. Shyness, in a more severe form, can be symptomatic of the various forms of perfectionism deeply entrenched in the personality that require considerable work to overcome. Shyness can be a tough problem for other reasons. There are some individuals who show evidence of signs of inhibition and withdrawal from other people shortly after birth, for no obvious reason, and who practice what appears to be a tendency to withdraw throughout most of their lives. They have to learn to act against the tendency by learning to become more relaxed and expressive in social situations.

A total assault on overcoming shyness is like a total assault in overcoming procrastination—much work is required. Also, some people will profit more rapidly than others. Since discussing all aspects of shyness would require another book, this section is limited to shyness that stems from fear.

A person who is characteristically shy feels fearful and inadequate in making social contacts and expects to be rejected when he does. This potential rejection is perceived as too painful to bear.

A typically shy-acting person may not be consistently shy, particularly on vacations when new friends seem easy to meet. During vacations and under similar relaxed circumstances, this person may come out of his shell and relate easily and enjoyably. This individual may also feel at ease and be quite gregarious with a few close friends. More typically, however, outside the familiar routine, the shy-acting person may be bashful and freeze with fear at social gatherings, as if saying, "People are to be feared; they can hurt; I'm not smart or attractive enough for anyone to be interested in; anyone who is interested in me has bad taste and can't themselves be worth talking to; if I say anything, I'll make a fool out of myself."

Preoccupied with these negative ideas about the self and anticipating rejection out of fear that others will hold the same opinion, these people sometimes appear to the casual observer as indifferent, disdainful, superior, cool, aloof, and distant. Some shy-acting people, however, appear as nervous and ill-at-ease as they feel inside. However the problem is behaviorally manifested, shy-acting persons typically have imaginative conjuring systems and tend to create mental myths or mind monsters with which they frighten and inhibit themselves.

I have already described some self-frightening ideas, such as "I'll make a fool out of myself" and that would be disastrous, so let's turn to some of the rationalizations that serve to cloak fear and to perpetuate this shyness problem. I will mention eight myths that I see most often. Be assured, there are many more.

- The myth of the perfect first impression—the conviction that disaster follows unless the person makes a perfect impression upon meeting someone for the first time. Naturally, hesitancy due to uncertainty ruins that perfect impression.

- The myth of the perfectly articulate person—the notion that one must refrain from expressing oneself unless one is sure to be highly articulate.

- The myth of the perfect opening gambit, as reflected in the statement "If I only knew how to start a conversation . . . ," which commonly distracts the person from starting a conversation.

- The myth of the perfect preparation—the belief that one cannot speak up in groups until one has totally digested the most popular novels and can insightfully analyze the most current news with full confidence.

- The myth that one must be completely comfortable and relaxed as a prerequisite to social interaction.

- The myth of the unassailable statement—the belief that in order to speak up one must be able to state ideas that transcend criticism.

- The myth of the savior—the hope that one will be rescued by a person who will take charge of one's life and protect one in social situations.

- The myth that one has to appear totally happy, free, and fun-loving in order to succeed socially.

## TACTICS FOR OVERCOMING SHYNESS

Now that some of the more common mental myths (rationalizations) have been exposed, here are some tactics you can use to deal with them:

- Identify and list the mental myths you suspect you may subscribe to.

- Use your imagination to create a mental picture of yourself as you would be socially behaving if you were free of each of these myths.

- Imagine yourself feeling a good sense of self-acceptance as you work to remove the myths from your life, and try to maintain this mental image.

Use direct confrontation techniques as aids in overcoming the myths. These myths and irrational belief-altering activities include:

- If you are afraid of expressing yourself in groups, try to speak up each time you are in a group until you overcome your discomfort (ask questions, make comments, ask someone to clarify a point).

- If you fear eating alone in a restaurant or going to a movie by yourself, face the fear by going alone.

- Carry or wear an object that could be a conversation piece. A comic button or the latest novel will do. When you display such objects, someone may feel inclined to initiate a conversation with you.

- Be alert to conversation pieces others may be displaying. Casually react to them, using the conversation piece as a start.

- Ask three strangers a day to tell you the exact time. Persist with this exercise until you feel at ease asking (use as your criterion: four consecutive days feeling relaxed asking).

- Practice acting friendly by saying "Hello" to people you barely know. Keep practicing until you feel natural greeting them.

- Try to maintain good eye contact with the people with whom you interact.

Develop a general plan for conquering shyness by doing the following:

- Identify those situations in which you are shy in which you'd like to stop acting shyly.
- Rank the items on the list from least to most difficult.
- Begin with the least difficult project on your list. Seek out or contrive situations where you can get practice dealing with this problem. For example, if the first (least difficult) situation on your list is going to unfamiliar department stores, enter and walk around such stores until that situation is no longer a problem. Then move to the next one. Occasionally, beginning with the top item in the list can have a ripple effect, making the less fearsome items easier to confront; if you feel up to it, start at the top of the list.

Improving your interpersonal skills involves developing not only positive behavioral but positive attitudinal skills as well. The attitudinal skills to develop involve objective thinking (see Chapter 9), recognizing and refuting your contingency thinking by seeking the facts. Behavioral skills involve experimenting with different ways of interacting with many different types of people.

As you work to develop both attitudinal and behavioral skills, sometimes you will feel discouraged, and you may backslide. Possibly, this retreat may occur when you first experientially "see" that you don't relate equally easily to all the people you want to relate to, regardless of how interpersonally skilled you become (generally, the people you will relate to best are those who have in common with you some basic morals, values, and interests). But bearing the discouragement and rebounding to continue with developing positive attitudinal and behavioral skills can be the pathway to interpersonal freedom.


## POSTSCRIPT

This chapter only scratches the surface of the number of people problems that one can possibly be personally confronted with. A few others are commitment anxieties, distrustfulness, and giving off bad "vibrations." Saddled with these problems, a person wishing to do so can adapt some concepts and exercises in this book as part of a self-help program or can work with a cognitive-behaviorally oriented counselor to develop such a program.

# Discomfort
# Dodging
# and
# Procrastination

*"Aside from physical danger,
is there anything else to
fear?"*

There is a proverb that says that if you give a man a fish, you feed him for a day; if you teach him how to fish, you feed him for the rest of his life.

Learning to tolerate discomfort is like learning to fish and is perhaps one of the most important lessons to learn on the trail of learning how to do it now. This is because so much needless psychological misery accrues from an unwillingness to accept the frustrations of daily living; and where there is an unwillingness to accept frustration, distress and procrastination follow.

Perhaps a comforting word from a friend will ease feelings of distress for the short term (like getting a free fish handout), but there is not always a friend in sight. So learning how to be a friend to oneself by learning to accept and tolerate discomfort is like learning how to fish. To help you learn this discomfort-tolerating process, I will describe various aspects of the need for comfort to heighten conceptual understanding, and I will suggest exercises to build emotional strength in accepting discomfort. The vehicles for this process will include methods for dealing with general discomfort, anxiety, depression, needs for immediate gratification, and methods for what to do when one hates to wait.

## LOOKING FOR THE EASY WAY

During the early 1950s, Abraham Low identified a "cult of comfort" whose membership deified comfort and indulged in an unwillingness to bear tension because of a fear of discomfort (tension, depression, inconvenience). Low pointed out, however, that the act of accepting discomfort has a profound effect upon the intensity of the discomfort—it becomes bearable and less threatening.

People can bear much more pain than they typically think they can. Prisoners of war have withstood enormous pressures and tortures to keep secrets from the enemy. Persons lost in the wilderness have borne great hardships and survived. So under conditions where a person seems entrapped in a perilous situation, with a sense of determination, the tension of the situation can be borne.

People can bear much pain and suffering for a cause they are determined to pursue. Recent studies in psychology have also shown that people can bear larger amounts of pain when they believe they can terminate the pain at any time. Thus persons hooked up to electrodes seem to tolerate electric shock better when they know they can push a button to terminate the shock. They realize they can control their circumstances, and that makes the pain more tolerable.

People who believe that they cannot control their psychological pain try to find their own "button" to insulate themselves from all distress, and "putting off" is typically that button. Yet these are the very people who ironically have the greatest pain and rarely accomplish what they are capable of accomplishing. In the clamor to divest themselves of all discomfort, they also divest themselves of satisfaction.

Achieving satisfaction and happiness in life is a prime desire of every human being. Each of us defines our source of satisfaction according to what has brought us the greatest pleasure or the keenest sense of accomplishment. Such pleasures may be anything—winning a chess tournament, dwelling in plush surroundings, communicating with a friend, finding a cure for cancer Some of these satisfactions can be attained with little investment; others require considerable work. Whether the investment is small or large, satisfaction is a common result of the human tendency to create and to construct.

Satisfaction seeking may become confused with the need for comfort, but they are not the same. Obtaining satisfaction requires making *efforts* that lead to goal attainment, and goal attainment often leads to satisfaction. Comfort seeking, on the other hand, involves the avoidance of effort or productive work and the substitution of a pursuit of a tension-free existence.

The very work necessary to achieve satisfaction may produce uncomfortable moments. So if one's main goal is comfort, one will tend to avoid initially unpleasant tasks that might ultimately culminate in satisfaction.

One way a person avoids satisfaction is by insisting that life must be comfortable. Such insistence predisposes a person to overreact to any source of displeasure or inconvenience, thereby creating more tension. The next step in this progression is an overdramatization of the severity of the situation. Anxious ruminations—telling oneself how horrible and unfair it is to be subjected to discomfort—help the discomfort escalate to sheer misery. Becoming preoccupied with this avoidable and escalated misery is a prime way of procrastinating.

The fear of discomfort partly comes from self-doubt when the person construes himself as too weak to withstand anxious or depressive feelings; this fear leads to discomfort dodging, which in turn leads to procrastination. Unfortunately, discomfort dodging can eventually culminate in more intensely negative feelings like guilt—because time passes, tasks are put off, one still has strong self-doubts, and in addition, one perceives oneself as a bad person for goofing off. As time is consumed on a guilt trip, the task is again put off and the avoidance cycle is repeated. The cycle can end in a sense of resignation: No matter what is done, the haunting feeling of guilt for avoiding the task is inescapable.

The comfort-seeking habit is a tough habit to overcome because most of us really dislike feeling uncomfortable, and there is often considerable resistance in going against one's own feelings. Part of this reluctance comes from believing that one has to follow one's feelings—if hungry, one eats; if tired, one sleeps.

There are obvious exceptions to these rules. People who are obese and want to lose weight need to suppress their urge to overeat. Like the overeater, a person who seeks membership in the comfort cult believes that he needs to give in to discomfort-avoiding whims. But the solution for the comfort seeker is the same as for the obese person—change requires restrictions.

## LEARNING TO BEAR DISCOMFORT

Start with the following exercises:

1. When you feel tense, "go with the feeling." The way you "go with the feeling" is to allow yourself to experience the feeling. Although you may fear the feeling of tension, choosing to experience rather than diverting from the feeling will allow you to gain a sense of "silent control."

2. You can teach yourself to bear discomfort by actively imagining situations you usually avoid. Think about a situation you find uncomfortable, like filling out your weekly report, doing

the dishes, or asking for a pay raise. If you start to feel uncomfortable, keep your attention glued to this feeling of discomfort. Now:

- o Try to determine where the feeling is localized (stomach, shoulders, legs, neck, chest, head).
- o Concentrate your attention on that tension zone.
- o If the feeling eludes you, try to bring it back by tightening that area of your body
- o Maintain the tension for ten minutes.

Chances are that when you conscientiously try to create a feeling of discomfort, you will familiarize yourself with your discomfort zone and this zone will feel less oppressive later. However, you may find that when you consciously try to create a feeling of discomfort, you can't. Indeed, the harder you try, the more comfortable you feel. You may even feel giddy. This is the *paradoxical effect*—you get the opposite of what you expect.

Teaching yourself to bear discomfort can be helped by solitary exercises. The procedure is as follows:

- Select a quiet room where you won't be disturbed for many hours.
- Remove all clocks and other timepieces from the room.
- Take the phone off the hook.
- Eliminate all other distractions, like newspapers, magazines, radios, and TV.
- Enter the room after lunch (around noon).
- Stay in the room until dusk (since you will not have a clock or watch, you will have to determine for yourself when dusk arrives).
- You may leave the room to go to the bathroom, but you must return to the room as quickly as you can.
- While you're in the room, your sole purpose is to experience yourself as alone. So you don't listen to the radio, fall asleep,

or write a letter. You just amuse yourself with your own thoughts.

- You may find yourself going through stages: like feeling initially uncomfortable, then finding your mind wandering, then feeling edgy and wanting to leave, then beginning to think about what you want to do with your life, then feeling relaxed.

- Plan (ahead of time) an activity for the end of the solitary exercise, one that involves people you like. You may find that you feel more relaxed with yourself and with others after completing the exercise.

Physical pain seems more acute at night and when there are fewer distractions. This is because a person experiencing physical pain more readily directs attention to this physical feeling. The same is true of emotional pain. Although there are good reasons to distract oneself from physical pain, there are also good reasons to avoid becoming emotionally enveloped. But with emotional stress, how one diverts oneself is paramount. One poor solution is to concentrate on "I've *got to* get rid of the feeling." This only escalates the problem. Another solution is to convince oneself that no problem exists. This form of denial rarely helps. A more workable solution is to consider *how to solve* the problem causing anguish. The following procedure may be helpful for organizing the "how-to":

- Describe the problem factually, e.g., "My fiancé(e) told me he or she was considering breaking the marriage engagement."

- Describe *what* you would *like* to see happen, e.g., "He or she resolved my doubts in favor of proceeding with the wedding."

- Describe *how* you would proceed to try to bring about the above result, assuming you were very tolerant of tension and discomfort, e.g., strongly expressing feelings of love and caring while simultaneously strongly supporting the fiancé(e)'s right to do what is best for him or her; allowing time to work at trying to identify and resolve problems related to the fiance(e)'s uncertainty; recognizing that getting "cold feet" is common just before a wedding

- Test your "how to's" and modify them with experience.

Another exercise involves discriminating between what you think is wise for you to do as opposed to what you feel an urge to do. For example, let's say that you want to give up smoking but crave a cigarette. Allow yourself to do what you think is wise by allowing yourself to build tolerance for tension by "going with" the feeling of craving rather than smoking.

In yet another exercise, you first identify five accomplishments you feel a sense of satisfaction about. Then take these steps:

- Examine the elements they have in common.
- Assess the *effort* they required.
- What are the possibilities today of extending one or more of the accomplishments?
- What can you do today to begin?
- Begin.

## ATTENDING TO OPPORTUNITY, NOT ANXIETY

To test a young man's worthiness to marry his daughter, a king confronted him with a difficult decision. Behind one door was the beautiful princess, behind the other, a tiger. The young man was faced with a choice between opportunity and certain death. Naturally, he was anxious.

Most choices in life do not have the tiger as a possible outcome. But some choices made between opportunity and image seem equally ominous. For example, Wilma went to a dance, and when she arrived she began to *anticipate* that no one would ask her to waltz, so she returned home. The possibility of not having a dance partner represented a danger to her psychological image ("ego"). The *thought* of sitting on the sidelines constituted the threat because she thought that she might be too homely and her personality too bland to attract a man, and as a consequence would remain sitting in the corner. Her self-doubts escalated to severe self-downing and she began to think that the people at the dance were noticing how isolated and how unworthy she was. A feeling of anxiety began to swell in her body and so she left.

Threats psychologically equivalent to the tiger behind the door ignited Wilma's sense of vulnerability. Thus Wilma doubted her ability to attract a dance partner and felt distressed because she anticipated danger, not opportunity. She saw the situation as one posing danger to her self-image rather than as an opportunity to meet new people and to develop her social skills. And it was just this focus on the possible danger to her self-worth that clouded her consciousness, making her blind to opportunity.

Wilma did not define her situation as a procrastination or avoidance problem. Indeed, she was so infected with her anxiety and her self-doubts that she could not see beyond her symptoms.

The symptoms of anxiety can be severe enough to command full attention on the part of those embroiled in attempting to eliminate the symptom. Some of these symptoms can be very startling. Acute anxiety, for example, usually involves symptoms like heart palpitations, sweating, tremor, shallow breathing, hyperventilation, flushing of the skin, and more. The symptoms can appear at a dance while fearing rejection, during an examination while anticipating failure, or choosing between two doors behind which are a tiger and a lady.

Not all anxiety has physically obvious symptoms. *Contained anxiety* may be characterized by a general sense of tenseness, apprehensiveness, worry, and behavioral rigidity. But whether contained or dramatically symptomatic, anxiety that continues over a long time span eventually may become so familiar and routine that one cannot imagine feeling differently; and the attention concentrated on the symptoms impedes awareness of the actual underlying problems, leaving the person feeling inadequate and helpless.

Much of healthy constructive living is put off when in a state of anxiety because a vicious double-troubles cycle frequently erupts.

Dwelling fearfully on tension increases the tension, and this emotional diversion blunts further awareness of underlying problems like self-doubt. So a person with a self-doubt problem may not see the problem because of the symptoms of anxiety. The symptoms, such as compulsive overeating (an action diversion), and the person's energy become tied to two levels of anxiety—the primary and the double-trouble, or secondary.

Double troubles frequently occur at night when a person lies in bed worrying about a problem. Since agonizing often causes a loss of sleep, the person may begin to worry about not sleeping. A solution is to command oneself to quit worrying and fall asleep. This won't work, and the problem escalates with added worry (anxiety) over being a "nervous wreck" in the morning, making mistakes on the job, and being reprimanded for making needless errors. This process, like the escalation process Wilma initiated for herself, is what Aaron Beck terms the *magnification process*.

People who think they need comfort are prone to magnify their problems when experiencing anxiety. Let's see what steps can be taken to abort this problem whenever it comes up.

## COMBATTING ANXIETY

People have active conjuring systems. They can anticipate crises or "tigers" for themselves that exist only in imagination. But if crises can be conjured up in fantasy, so can opportunities be anticipated. Thus, when you are worried about something, like being rejected at a social gathering, try also to look for the best opportunities. Then decide *how to* make those opportunities actualities. Test out your plan.

Escalating anxiety can be combatted by a technique of *humorous exaggeration*. In humorous exaggeration you purposely exaggerate, through imagination, the situation you are anxious about. So if you feel uptight about getting a report completed on time, take the consequences to a humorous extreme. For instance, imagine your boss jumping out of his clothing at the news that the report is late, and then reporting you to the United Federation of Planets. Then the starship *Enterprise* whisks you away to a galaxy far away and places you in a penal colony staffed by people who actively procrastinate. Pretend your sentence in the penal colony is one week, and near the end of the week you try to get the staff to start processing papers for your release. Humorous exaggeration can help reduce that "uptight" feeling.

When you feel anxious, you tend to make an emotional dwarf of yourself.* You tell yourself "horror stories" about your inabilities, thus paint a small, restrictive mental picture of yourself. Fortunately, you are rarely as restricted as you think you are. So when you are anxious, sit back and try to expand that mental picture of you to include a picture of you trying to do your darndest to do your best and watch that dwarf grow. Consider alternative ways of doing your best and play out each alternative in fantasy. This positive fantasy trip adds ways to expand your awareness of your possibilities, and thus creates an expanded self-picture.

## DEPRESSION AND PROCRASTINATION

Like Joe Btfsplk in the *Li'l Abner* comic strip, people who feel depressed act as if they had a cloud of gloom hanging over their heads. They have a sense of dejection, hopelessness, and helplessness. They pity themselves and believe they are neither able to stand the discomfort they are experiencing nor tolerate the discomfort they anticipate experiencing if they are to try to get better. They tend to feel listless and are inclined to avoid responsibilities.

Some depressions are physiological in nature and result from a biochemical imbalance. The imbalance fosters a listless feeling

---

*Sometimes a person who dwarfs himself through self-effacing thoughts later tries to build a new image by bragging. It is important to counter false build-ups as well as false shrinkings.

that the person often *interprets* to mean he is without energy and thus severely hampered and doomed to ineptness. Depression can also be psychological and triggered by an external event, like the loss of a job. Psychological depression is self-generated through self-doubts, self-downing, and/or intolerance of tension. In the primary psychological depressions, the depressed person tends to heed a little voice within that repeats the equivalent of the following:

- My situation is hopeless.
- I am helpless to do anything.
- It's unfair that I have to feel this way.
- The effort that I will need to pull myself out of this malaise is just too much for me.
- Poor me. Why do I always have to be the one to suffer?
- I can't stand this tension.

A person giving in to this "little voice" feels increasingly hopeless and helpless. Sometimes the person simultaneously feels angry at himself and blames the outside world. In any event, the person who feels depressed perpetuates the discomfort of depression because of the belief that the effort needed to pull out of the quagmire of depression will only produce more pain. Paradoxically, most people who feel depressed actually have an abundance of contained energy that can be released to fight the depression and the procrastination generating from the depression.

## OVERCOMING PROCRASTINATION DUE TO DEPRESSION

Even though awareness–action methods of countering depression can help substantially, not all depression is alterable by such methods. Clinical depressions characterized by loss of reality contact because of severe biochemical imbalance require special treatment, and psychopharmacologists are the specialists to see. However, psychological depressions and most mild-to-moderate physiological depressions can be reduced by self-help methods. The following are a few suggestions:

- William James has suggested a method of dealing with depression. As James himself suffered from many bouts with this problem, he speaks from personal experience. James notes that depression is not continuous. From time to time your attention shifts momentarily from your depression. When this happens, you can use this brief interval to assert your will to mobilize and move yourself.

- The how-to technique, helpful in dealing with general discomfort dodging and anxiety, can be applied to depression. Rather than wallow in thoughts of helplessness, hopelessness, and self-pity, identify the problem(s) you face and think about how to solve it (them). Next, actively test your plan.

- Can't seem to muster enough energy to use the how-to plan? Try scrubbing your bathtub with a toothbrush. Chances are that the how-to plan will appear more appealing. Now, this may appear on the surface to be a silly solution; however, it works in many cases. Either because the toothbrush task proves tedious and most other tasks are viewed as pleasant by comparison or because the activity breaks the depressive stream of consciousness, this method usually helps.

- A method to contradict the "little voice" subverting you into further depression is to allow yourself to focus momentarily on happy thoughts or images: Think about one thing that you did well today, or how nice it would be to take a hot shower. Next, use this change of focus to mobilize yourself into an activity that you might enjoy: Call a friend, take a walk, read a poem, observe a beautiful work of art or nature. Allow yourself to really "get into" whatever activity you choose. Chances are that this mobilization into an enjoyable activity will further counteract your depression because (a) such enjoyment will spur you to think of happy (rather than sad and hopeless) thoughts; (b) you will have counteracted your discomfort-dodging tendency; and (c) you will have demonstrated through your own actions that you are *not* helpless or hopeless and that you can work yourself out of depression.

## HATING TO WAIT

Richard had a most miserable problem. It seems that his tension tolerance was very low, and he thought he had to have what he wanted when he wanted it in order to avoid tension. Because of his demands for immediate gratification, he often acted against his own enlightened self-interest. For example, one day he decided to buy new furniture. Surveying his possible choices, he located some pieces he really liked. Unfortunately, those pieces could not be delivered for six weeks. So he decided to order furniture that had slight appeal but could be delivered the following day so as to satisfy his desire to fill some space in his apartment. On another occasion he varnished a set of bookshelves for his wall. He hurried through the varnishing so that he could see the completed job, and while the bookcase was still very sticky, he picked it up and positioned it against the wall so that he could see how it looked. Then he was saddled with the unpleasant job of redoing the shelves in order to cover his finger marks.

Richard's rushing is a form of procrastination, as the rushing results in putting off working to achieve quality.

Ann was very careful and efficient in writing letters to friends and often planned vacations months in advance. However, social engagements were her nemesis, as the following episode illustrates: Ann and Roger have been married for three years. As usual, we find Roger pacing the floor while Ann hurriedly applies her makeup. The time is 8:15 P.M., and they are already fifteen minutes late for dinner at the Johnsons'. Although Roger and Ann live ten minutes away, they arrive breathlessly at 9:00 P.M. and receive a cool welcome from the Johnsons and their other guests.

During the trip to the Johnsons', the couple vociferously argue about showing up late for dinner. Ann denies her lateness is a problem, as Roger shouts, "You're keeping everyone waiting, damn you!" Ann loudly counters: "I would be embarrassed if I didn't look my best. We can't have the Johnsons thinking poorly of us, and that's just what they would think if I didn't look my best! Besides, I hate to wait around, waiting for dinner to be served. I can't stand being bored."

Hating to wait is a problem that many people experience as impatience, and impatiently requiring immediate gratification can become especially acute when one decides to rid oneself of the *problem* of impatience. Very often the person afflicted with this problem is inclined to be impatient with himself and to add stress and discouragement by believing: "Because I've suffered so long with this problem of feeling impatient and stressed, I must resolve it immediately. I've suffered long enough!"

Normally, a lifetime of impatience is not reversed by a declaration to change, nor is it reversed by the "I've suffered enough" argument. Demanding immediate freedom from discomfort (impatience) has about the same effect as screaming at oneself to fall asleep when one is wide awake.

"Rushing" to satisfy one's whims and delaying are flip sides of a coin molded from intolerance for tension. Rushing to avoid tension is like putting something off to avoid tension—both forms of avoidance lead to greater tension. Both ways of avoiding discomfort—rushing and procrastinating—often prove to be annoying habits. Fortunately, they are habits that can be broken.

## LEARNING TO WAIT

There are many ways to gain skill in learning to *delay* gratification. Pick several delay strategies from the following list that seem to be most helpful and try them. (Isn't it odd that in a book on reducing delays we'd be talking about increasing delays!)

- When eating a meal, take small bites and place your eating utensils on the table between bites.

- When feasible, have dessert fifteen minutes after completing your meal.
- Plan a vacation nine months in advance. Make your travel arrangements and sit back and wait.
- Complete a novel you once found interesting, but may have only half-read.
- Start a hobby, like needlepoint, that requires time and con- centration to do well.
- Plan your morning schedule so that you can comfortably arrive ten minutes early for work.
- Put off your after-breakfast cigarette until after lunch.
- Systematically put a predetermined amount of money into your savings account each payday.
- Take fifteen minutes before bed to prepare for the next day.
- Go for a three-hour stroll through a familiar area (your neighborhood, the local pond, the botanical gardens). Develop your observational skills by studying what you have not observed before.
- Take the same stroll and develop your observational skills by studying what you have observed before.
- Obtain a leaf. Study the leaf for six hours. During that time explore the leaf in as many sensory ways as you can. Note the many sensory qualities that are readily apparent. Then, when you think you have come to the end of your creative potential, try to discover fifty more.
- Write a one-page story about the leaf. Revise your story six times. Write your last revision just to amuse yourself.
- Be early for appointments with friends. Bring a book along to read if you have to wait.
- Buy birthday cards today for friends' and relatives' upcoming birthdays in the next year. Sign the cards, stamp and address the envelopes, and mail each out two weeks before the birthday.

If there are no items in this list you believe would help, or if you have a project you think would be particularly helpful to do, substitute your own project.

Hating to wait has many possible causes other than pure discomfort dodging:

- *Fated-to-Fail*. This is the erroneous belief that whatever you do, you're doomed to fail. (So what difference does it make if you show up late?) It also includes the belief that you'd better play it very safe in your life because unless you are careful, you may be wiped out.

- *Rebellion*. You may show up late, not so much because you hate to wait, but because you are tired of being told to show up on time.

- *Testing*. You show up late because you want to test others' tolerance and to see if you will be able to gain their attention.

- *Agoraphobia*. You're afraid of leaving the sanctuary of your home and therefore wait until the last possible minute to leave.

- *Mistiming*. You have a habit of expecting too much from yourself. In other words, you consistently underestimate the amount of time it will take you to prepare to leave.

See if any of the above motives operate in your hate-to-wait problem. If so, make up a how-to plan to counteract these problems.

Sometimes a preview experience can be instructive in illustrating the advantages of patience. A *preview experience* is when you act the way you want to act upon one occasion. For example, you are normally very late for parties, but one day you arrive on time and feel good about your accomplishment. You are delighted with the change and expect that the change will be durable. Actually, the change most probably is a good illustration of how your life can improve *if* you sustain the change. That's why the experience was a preview experience. A positive preview experience is particularly helpful, as it constitutes a strong cue signaling the possibility for change. Imagine experiencing a tension-free moment after having been chronically anxious. Clearly, the preview experience can help establish a positive experiential referent to work toward attaining more regularly.

# Six Procrastination Styles: A Fresh Look at an Old Problem

"The daisy looks different from every angle,
but it remains the same."

A group of friends and I once took a series of karate lessons
with a talented Korean instructor who spoke broken English. One
day the instructor was teaching us how to defend against an assailant who grabs one's shirt or suit jacket. To demonstrate, he asked
me to grab his karate jacket, and as I did so he skillfully bent my
thumb inward, easily bringing me to the floor. Next, he grabbed
my karate jacket. As I fumbled around, engrossed in grasping his
left thumb, he adeptly drew back his right fist and positioned

himself to clobber me. When I finally looked up to see what was happening, I heard the instructor say, "Many way do same thing." He had taught his lesson well!

In the spirit of "many way do same thing," in this chapter we'll look at the procrastination problem from a different angle. Just as there are a number of methods for disarming an assailant, there are many ways to view the procrastination phenomenon. When developing a means of attacking a problem, it is always helpful to have a variety of tactics from which to choose. Toward this end, six different procrastination styles are presented here: mental procrastination, drifting, behavioral procrastination, frustrated artistry, competitiveness, and intrigue creating.

## MENTAL PROCRASTINATION

One type of procrastination pattern is putting off thinking about how to solve personal problems. People whose style is that of *mental procrastination* often comment upon how unhappy they are, focus too hard on trying to rid themselves of negative feelings, and routinely repeat procrastination patterns. They suffer from disorganized thinking, obsessive ruminations, and indecisiveness. Here is an example:

Walter suffers from a bad case of omphaloskepsis—contemplating his navel. On a typical evening we can find him sitting listlessly in his apartment ruminating about his old friends and all the fun he used to have. He plays his favorite old songs on the stereo, practices a few outmoded dance steps, and imagines himself a Byronic hero, sweeping some beautiful, breathtaking young maiden off her feet. But alas, these are pipe dreams. Walter's old friends have long since married and moved away. Nowadays Walter rarely socializes. On those few occasions when he gets out of his apartment, covers his navel, and makes an attempt to meet new people, Walter returns home feeling discouraged and forlorn because his aloof, silent, macho glare has again failed to attract the fair damsel, or even the not-so-beautiful wallflower. During his work day, Walter maintains the same "Woe is me" posture, hiding in his cubicle to avoid having lunch with colleagues who he thinks are unfriendly bores. So Walter spends his days and nights feeling bitter and thinking how cruel is the world and how unfriendly are the people in it. Why should he even try?

Walter mentally procrastinates. He puts off identifying his real problems and developing solutions to them. He won't admit to himself that he actually is afraid of people and fears that others will find him unacceptable. Instead, he spends his energy on fantasy and blames the rest of the world for his problems.

### How to Detect and Change a Style of Mental Procrastination

Mental procrastination reflects a style of blocking problems from awareness. Thus, the first and most crucial step in the process of change is to unmask the real problems underlying the mental blockage. This is difficult, but certainly possible. So if you think you may be mentally procrastinating to blot out your real problems and to avoid facing them, try the following exercises:

- Write your autobiography. Use as stimuli old photographs from different periods in your life. Try to remember colors, smells, textures, and other sensory impressions from various periods of your life to help stimulate you to recall additional experiences. Ask friends and relatives to recount memorable anecdotes about you. Once you have completed your personal history, look closely for gaps—things that you may have once wanted to do that are conspicuously absent from your history. Also, look for dead-end patterns—things you once started that were never accomplished. Lastly, look for anxious or otherwise uncomfortable times where problems emerged which were never resolved. Finding these can help you uncover areas of blockage.

- Use your complaints and procrastinating as a red flag to signal troublespots that you can then examine for discomfort dodging and/or self-doubt.

- Discuss with an objective, fair-minded listener what your problems are and what you can do about them.

## DRIFTING

*Drifting*, a first cousin to mental procrastination, has been succinctly described by Karen Horney. Drifting involves a pattern of routinely failing to identify life objectives. In my experience people who drift tend to have only vague and indiscriminate goals and plans. As a consequence, such a person either feels hounded by thoughts of purposelessness or blocks feelings of sadness, remorse, or barrenness. Furthermore, this person tends to act blandly and indifferently toward life. Rather than initiating, this drifting style is one of *reacting* to life's happenings, and the person who drifts mostly settles for what life has to offer rather than selecting what he or she wants. Here is an example of the drifting style:

George is a security guard at the Third National Bank. He's a bright, sensitive man who "drifts" along doing a job he is over-qualified for—one that he secretly loathes. He feels stalemated and stagnated because he can't think of what other job he would prefer doing. At times he worries about his future and what his life will be like later. He feels a sense of aimlessness or purposelessness, and this sense adds to his worries. He feels trapped in what the existentialists describe as a vacuum of meaninglessness. Indeed, he is not even sure what his problem is. Occasionally, however, he has a dim awareness that he doesn't seem to make commitments easily, is confused, and seems to be without direction.

### Dealing with Drifting

The key word in disrupting drifting is *commitment*. The big question is: commitment to *what*? So the first step in disrupting drifting is to make an appraisal of your current situation and ascertain what you would like to have that you feel is presently lacking in your life.

Drifting is an evasion of responsibility. So when you drift, you tend to act irresponsibly toward yourself. Working to take yourself more seriously—viewing yourself as a person worthy of caring for—can be a way to initiate responsibility. One way to do this is to assess your strengths so as to better see your positive qualities. This task can be readily accomplished by examining activities that you perform well. For example, if you play bridge skillfully, examine the qualities that contribute to your bridge skills: good memory, strategic sense, judgment, intelligence, concentration, good communication. By examining several activities (like bridge), you'll begin to recognize qualities that keep repeating themselves—qualities you value. In using this strength analysis for developing self-awareness and self-evaluation, you may find yourself developing greater self-respect. Furthermore, knowledge of your skills and qualities may provide you with a basis for determining career and interpersonal objectives and provide a basis for making a commitment to yourself for advancing yourself.

## BEHAVIORAL PROCRASTINATION

*Behavioral procrastination* is a very deceptive style in which an organizational system is developed and plans for action are made, but implementation of the plans is put off. The person whose style is behavioral procrastination avoids possible discomfort and tension associated with the actual follow-through process by not following through. In the following example, you'll see just how this works.

At first glance Sally appears to be one of those utterly organized, efficient people whom we all envy. Outwardly, she seems to really have her act together. She methodically decides what she wants and how to get it. For example, recently she has obtained books and other information about setting up a fresh-water aquarium, passed the real-estate-broker's exam, and formulated a step-by-step plan to get a promotion and raise in pay at her job. Her office desk and apartment are so marvelously organized that she can find anything at a moment's notice. She has a huge calendar bearing appointments, outings, parties, and birthdays for the upcoming year. As she arises each morning, Sally makes a long, annotated list of things to do during the day and approximate times for each activity. The big catch in this organizational genius is that she rarely gets anything done. She constantly distracts herself with a myriad of projects and plans, and becomes so preoccupied in the planning that she fails to follow through. Thus, an empty aquarium tank sits neatly in a corner to be used at some later date, her plans for career advancement drift into the recesses of her brain, her friends and relatives rarely get a birthday card from Sally, and the daily list of things to do doesn't get done.

### Beating Behavioral Procrastination

Underlying behavioral procrastination loom well-hidden fears and self-doubts as well as a strong urge to avoid the uncomfortable. If you use a style of behavioral procrastination, the following exercises will help you to fend off the psychological foes that support this procrastination style:

- Recognize that behavioral procrastination is a tough problem.
- To build awareness, look for cues—projects or tasks that you have put time and effort into planning but have put off implementing.
- Introspect to see if self-doubts are hampering your progress. For example, if you were to follow through with your plans, are you afraid that your work would not be perfect?
- Introspect to see if you aren't believing in "magic." For example, do you believe follow-through should be effortless?
- Assess what your alternatives to self-doubt or magical wishes are and act on the alternative you believe best helps the implementation of your plans.
- People who behaviorally procrastinate typically use any sign of bodily fatigue as a rationalization for resting. Instead of allowing yourself to rest, push yourself to your limits on some

action you've planned doing. Unless you are ill or physically disabled, you can push your body quite a bit. You'll probably find that your limits are much higher than you had imagined.

## THE FRUSTRATED ARTIST

The style of the *frustrated artist* is that of cultivating doubts about ability instead of following creative urges and developing creative talents.

The artist's talents don't necessarily have to be as robust and bountiful as those of a Leonardo da Vinci or a William Shakespeare. The quality and dollar value are unimportant. What is of concern is that those inner urges are denied expression and that such suppression leads to needless frustration and restraint.

The frustration and restraint of the suppressed artist take many forms: the child who wants to play but must behave; the woman who feels like laughing and telling jokes but refrains because she thinks such behavior is undignified; the teenager who wants to sing in the shower but is afraid to sing off key; the first-rate writer who comes in second because he won't let go of conventional style. All are frustrated artists, even if their work will never win prizes or be displayed at the Metropolitan Museum of Art.

Frustrated artists avoid the very activity they enjoy. They put off their art and instead wander in a mire of uncertainty, wondering what to do with their free time. This is their eternal problem—avoiding decisions out of fear of error, renewing self-doubts.

The frustrated artist waits in the same old, well-known corner of restricted existence, rarely risking the frustration and tension that might accompany the real expression of inner feelings. The frustrated artist avoids learning the important lesson that self-expression, despite possible attendant frustration, is a liberating, self-fulfilling experience.

The creative pursuit is not a hobby or avocation; it is a lifelong process that can constantly open new experiences for the individual to explore and enjoy. Through these creative channels, the artist unbinds the chains of subservience to the ideas of others in order to think and plan with enlightened independence. Even if you don't completely identify with our frustrated-artist style, you may procrastinate because of similar restraints. Let's see what you can do to start liberating yourself.

### Spring Yourself Loose

The secret of breaking loose from the chains of suppression is through involvement.

- Involve yourself in memories of times when you expressed inner awareness and felt that your outer expressions were constructively congruent with your inward feelings or ideas. Do this and you have a point of reference for what it feels like to be so involved.

- From the first exercise, extract the modality of expression you used: writing, acting, painting, singing, organizing, counseling, talking, diagnosing, or whatever. Create a situation in which you can involve yourself in the very artistic activities you've denied yourself. Pick a time of the day, each day, when you will involve yourself in your creative project. Persist even if you feel discouraged. Many artists, like baseball players, go into slumps periodically. Many artists report fears of running out of ideas, so there is no reason why you should be different.

- Select a mentor or ally who can help you improve your skill. Artists are born, but the skill or technical competency needs developing, and that skill is necessary to give full expression to that which is within.

## THE COMPETITIVE
## PROCRASTINATION STYLE

Jack is aggressively competitive. He sees even casual conversations as opportunities to have a contest to prove his superiority. However, rather than compete with people who are equal to his ability, he competes with people who are clearly less capable than he. He subsequently spends much time congratulating himself for his victories. Jack plays what Stephen Potter terms one-upmanship games. He tries to upstage and show that he is smarter. He believes this style of interacting makes him a stronger person.

Jill, on the other hand, associates competitiveness with aggressiveness. She is afraid of appearing nonfeminine if she expresses her competitive desires. But more importantly, she is very much afraid that exposing her talents will cause others to aggressively retaliate. Fearful of this presumed retaliation, she avoids expressing herself.

Like Jack, Jill compares her abilities with the talents of others. And this compulsion to compare is what I term *comparitivitis*. People who suffer from comparitivitis are quite competitive people.

Comparitivitis is not only in evidence when one compulsively compares—favorably or unfavorably—one's qualities with those of others, but also when a person internally creates "time-performance" standards and anticipates that his *actual* performance will fail to equal the standard. In other words, the person establishes nearly impossible time standards. Such time misjudgments then lead to procrastination because rather than risk failure in meeting the standard, the project is put off. Thus the person involved in this self-competitive style suffers from *shoulditis*. Here the person believes he *should* continually be able to work at top speed and there *should* be no blocks to progress. The naturally talented writer who doesn't write because he can't write a great book every week illustrates the extremes of this self-defeating process.

Shoulditis and comparitivitis are mental viruses. They are mental viruses because they invade the conceptual system and weaken judgment. In addition to weakening judgment, they have other side effects: distraction, tension, and procrastination.

Competitive procrastination styles often lead to boredom, which often sets the stage for an urge for stimulation. This urge for stimulation, however, is often concentrated in nonproductive games of the Stephen Potter variety. The most serious consequence of this style, however, is that the competitor learns little about himself because of the repetitive nature of the games and because of the limited opportunity to discover and to test his productive talents.

There is clear advantage to a healthy "competitive spirit." In contrast to the competitive procrastination style, a healthy competitive spirit directed at building rather than comparing leads to growth, efficiency, and productivity. In the following section we will examine ideas and concepts that can help turn about a competitive procrastination style.

## GETTING ON TO A PRODUCTIVE STYLE

Creating and engaging in *productive challenges* channels mental, emotional, and physical energies in the direction of healthy functioning. These productive challenges can take the form of engaging in activities that have previously been avoided, such as:

- creating a new theory
- learning to ride a bicycle
- reciting poetry in public
- creating a statue from clay
- mastering a game like bridge
- building a doll house (or a real house)
- remodeling furniture
- developing skill in acting or singing
- learning to play a musical instrument
- becoming skillful in speaking a foreign language
- attending or teaching classes on a topic of interest
- coordinating a volunteer program
- making concrete plans for a business expansion

- developing active listening skills
- practicing self-expression in a group or with an individual
- creating a new organizing system

It has been my observation that people periodically require new challenges. If these challenges are healthy and are attempted, the person learns more about his strengths and capabilities. And this concrete, experience-derived information feeds into a healthy self-concept.

New productive challenges are important; however, their value is sometimes dissipated through procrastination. Procrastination, like a weed in a garden, periodically becomes a problem. However, like pulling weeds to save the garden, if procrastination is dealt with swiftly by returning to the challenge, like the farmer who gets more tomatoes for his weeding efforts, the person returning and sticking to the challenge gains expanded self-knowledge and more competencies for his efforts.

On comparitivitis—naturally it is better to concentrate on doing the best you can do rather than *having* to be better than anyone else. I find it useful to keep in mind that unlike a foot race, which has only one winner, life provides many ways for many people to win in both similar and different ways. And although it is certainly wise to plan time to get a job done, and wise forecasting helps improve planning, in the final analysis, the time that is required to get a job completed is the time that it takes.

## INTRIGUE CREATING 6

*Intrigue creating*, the sixth procrastination style, involves making a decision today that creates a crisis later—a crisis that the intrigue creator must invest considerable time to resolve. For example, deciding to put off paying the telephone bill results in a shut-off crisis several weeks later—a needless hassle that drains considerably more time and energy than would have been expended if the bill were paid on time. Some students have developed the intrigue-creating style into a fine art: They cut classes, goof off during the semester, then come up with a stupendous excuse for enticing a professor into giving a makeup exam or giving an extension on that research paper. The plot for this suspense is defying authority, testing the professor's tolerance limits, and flexing one's skill in turning a bad situation around to one's advantage. And this intrigue has all the stimulating elements of a come-from-behind victory.

A person may also play the suspense game by threatening his collaborator with quitting in the middle of a project, as a means of stimulating long, dramatic discussions to resolve the crisis. In all cases the intrigue-creating (crisis-creating) pattern involves risk and some danger and is generally initiated to create a sense of excitement and a feeling of stimulation.

Stimulating as intrigues may be, they are actually mere diversionary activities. Energies invested in intrigue are shifted away from purposeful, constructive activities that could in themselves provide a source of stimulation and excitement.

## Productive Stimulation

The following are ways of ridding oneself of intrigue-creating behavior:

- When making a decision to put something off, first pause to check the long-term effects of that decision. Could the decision, for example, end in an unnecessary crisis? This *stop–check* technique, used consistently, helps to make clear the impact that putting things off may have.

- Intrigue creating not only reflects a need for stimulation, but also a fear of failure. It is therefore important to examine why you think you need the sort of stimulation that is derived from intrigues and what it is that you are afraid of failing at.

- Intrigue creating sometimes involves an attempt to get a quick emotional charge. Threatening to quit a job or absolve a relationship may provide that quick charge. As a constructive alternative, ascertain the important and worthwhile challenges facing you and pursue them. You'll still get that energizing spark, and the consequences will be positive.

## ENACTMENT EXERCISES TO ALTER YOUR PROCRASTINATION STYLE

One way to get rid of a procrastination style is to replace it with an antiprocrastination style. Using this technique, a drifter, for example, would develop and enact a new role of systematically making and following through on life goals. No matter what your current style of procrastination, you can formulate and act out a new role for yourself. By doing so, you will have moved a long way toward getting it done.

The idea of role enactment is not a new one. J. L. Moreno developed the role-playing technique as part of his psychodrama model of therapy. Behavioral therapists have used and still do use contemporary role-playing techniques to help their clients develop effective communication skills. George Kelly has modified the role-playing technique in the development of his fixed-role therapy model—a model that can be used effectively to break out of an old procrastination style and into a new style of getting it done. Here's how:

First, write an autobiographical sketch (see the list following the heading "How to Detect and Change a Style of Mental Procrastination," earlier in this chapter, for suggestions on how to write your autobiography). Next, examine your sketch closely for "points of immobilization" (areas of procrastination). Once you have isolated these stumbling blocks, use them to write a new script for yourself—one in which you have eliminated the stumbling blocks (or points of immobilization) and replaced them with purposeful actions. For instance, if one of your stumbling blocks was avoiding expressing your opinions at executive board meetings, you would create a new script in which you clearly and forcefully express your opinions at such meetings. Before writing your new script (role),

read over the following guidelines that Kelly suggests for constructing your new role:

- Write biographical sketches and new role scripts as objectively as possible. When composing your script, use the third
  person ("he," "she,") as if someone else were doing the writing.
- Make the new script much more than a modification or minor
  adjustment of your biographical sketch. Make the new role the
  antithesis of your old pattern of behavior, and write it to
  completely reverse the points of immobilization.
- Write the new script with an awareness of how the new role
  will affect other people. Specifically design the role so that the
  impact on others is constructive.
- An effective new role is one that is flexible and realistic.
- Act out the new role as if it were an experiment or a make-
  believe exercise.
- To add to the make-believe element of the new role, make up
  a new name for yourself. (Naturally, keep the new name a
  secret.)

Kelly points out that there is no concrete formula for writing the
new role script. Ingenuity is left to the writer.

In addition to Kelly's suggestions, the following list contains
items you may want to include in developing your new life script:

- style of clothing
- manner of speaking to bosses (tone of voice, content)
- manner of speaking to colleagues (businesslike, cordial,
  friendly)
- manner of speaking to strangers (upbeat, neutral, friendly)
- body posture (express confidence)
- use of leisure time

- manner of handling problems
- reaction to criticism
- reaction to negativism on the part of others
- types of risks taken
- opportunities sought
- style of interacting in groups
- manner of expressing feelings
- future plans
- energy level
- awareness of others' feelings
- manner of getting work done
- relations with members of the opposite sex
- relations with same-sex friends
- interests
- values
- main beliefs

Now write your new script. Test it. Modify it. Live it.

**9**

# Clear Thinking Helps Get It Done

"The situation changes in the mind of the observer."

Joseph K. in Franz Kafka's *The Trial* was arrested one morning and was never told the reason why. Although he was released on his own recognizance to await trial, his life revolved around trying to discover what charges were brought against him and how his defense was progressing.

Many people who procrastinate place themselves on psychological trial daily. They act as if they suffered from some unknown but fatal personality flaw and go on searching for this flaw in much the same way that Joseph K. searched for the reason for his indictment. Unfortunately, awareness of underlying personality strengths is blurred because of the self-deceptive entanglements that exist in the psychological jungle. And so the search goes on among the entanglements for the fatal "flaw."

Various inaccuracies in thinking lead to reality distortions that can lend credence to one's personality "flaw" theory. Such faulty thinking takes many forms other than the diversionary and contingency forms I have already described. The triggers for emotional problems, these faulty thought patterns include: faulty evaluations, extremist thinking (exaggerations), and mental vagueness (unclear abstractions, overgeneralizations).

According to the semanticist Alfred Korzypski, such faulty thinking can lead to emotional disturbance, and straightening out faulty thinking can lead to emotional health. From my experience, straight thinking can clear out most reasons for procrastinating.

Knowing the pitfalls that interfere with straight thinking is often insufficient to clear up that thinking and change procrastination patterns. More is needed. First and most obvious, change requires effort: One has to know more than how to exercise in order for the benefits of exercise to build muscle and endurance; one actually has to exercise to gain the benefits. One must also be able to adapt to changing circumstances to maintain the benefits. The same is largely true for thinking straight. Wendel Johnson makes this point clear when he states:

> What most fundamentally characterizes the scientific, or well adjusted, or highly sane person is not chiefly the particular habits that he holds, but rather the deftness with which he modifies them or responds to changing circumstances. He is set to change, in contrast to the more rigid, dogmatic, self defensive individual who is set to "sit tight."

So straight thinking requires technical knowledge, practice, and flexibility.

Productive thinking and acting, a result of mental flexibility, allows one to maintain a realistic perspective. Indeed, if there is one condition most conducive to productivity, it is a good perspective.

A realistic perspective and procrastination are an unusual mix. Moreover, a realistic perspective crowds out the mental entanglements found in the Kafka-style intrigues. To help this healthy crowding process, the following discussion indicates how to begin to think clearly and to develop perspective.

## FAULTY EVALUATIONS

*Faulty evaluations* take many forms and can lead to stress and procrastination. For example, a faulty evaluation, such as "My life is hopeless and I don't have the capacity to change it," if believed, leads to immobilizing feelings of depression. The mañana belief "Tomorrow is a better day to work" directly leads to subtle stress and procrastination.

Knowing about the interwoven complexity of thought, feelings, and actions can have profound value in helping you to unravel your mental entanglements, free your emotions, and get it done. To illustrate how this knowledge can help, I'll describe a case from my psychotherapy files.

One of my clients had chronic headaches. She had been to a number of physicians who prescribed every known medication to help alleviate her pain—alas, to no avail. She suffered despite the medication. When I first saw her, she presented herself as an exceptionally demanding person, preoccupied with a need for people to act fairly and politely toward her. Such a demanding attitude creates inner tension, so I pointed this out to her and tried to show her how her attitude could contribute to her headaches. She denied that her thinking was faulty, and even if it were, she claimed, it could not cause headaches. To test this hypothesis, we tried an experiment. For the experiment the client agreed to drive her car in heavy traffic on Madison Avenue in New York City for fifteen minutes and to try to be aware of her thoughts, feelings, and actions. She was specifically assigned to write down thoughts she had when she started to feel herself become tense and to note the situation she was in when experiencing such tense feelings.

Twenty minutes later, the client returned to my office and pointed out that she was amazed with the revelation that she did indeed talk to herself. She excitedly noted that the first time a cab driver swung into the lane directly in front of her, she tensed up and caught herself mentally cursing the cabbie as she tensed. Furthermore, she became clearly aware that she was telling herself that cab drivers should act with courtesy, and the more she thought that way, the more tense and headachey she felt. When she recognized what she was doing to herself, she began to view the whole episode as silly. She actually changed her ideas about cabbies from condemnation to a jovial recognition that the cabbie's action was typical of other cabbies' actions: It was a reflection of the "nature of the New York beast." With the "nature of the beast" idea dominating, she noticed that her headache had disappeared. This client needed no more convincing. She saw the thought/feeling/action relationship.

During the next week, she recorded her thoughts, feelings, and actions, isolating thought patterns contributing to her stress. The experiment paid great dividends as a consequence of her conscientious self-observations. This awareness, combined with a concerned attempt to look at a situation from more than one perspective, had the effect of significantly reducing her tension and headaches.

Not all cases end this happily. Procrastination problems, in particular, are normally more resistant to change. Procrastination habits are hard to change mainly because the relationship between thoughts, feelings, and actions is clouded by rigid defenses that reduce awareness of self-doubts and fears of discomfort. Therefore, it is important to examine these defenses and try to replace them with a healthy, productive problem-solving outlook.

Defenses serve to block the development of productive thinking in three ways. One way that can block awareness of your problem is by *externalizing blame*. That is, you can claim that your procrastination is due to the unrealistic scheduling demands of society. Or you can block awareness by turning inwardly and *struggling to gain control* of yourself so as to avoid discomfort and promote perfection. This tactic hardly ever works, because when you continue insisting that you must maintain control, you've already lost control. The third tactic is *indifference* (neutralizing). You take your procrastination problem as insignificant, or you deny having a problem (when you most certainly do!). As a part of your self-help scheme, it is important to determine if you are an externalizer, internalizer, or neutralizer—or some combination of the three.

If you are an externalizer, your faulty ideas often center upon exempting yourself from responsibility by blaming others or circumstances. Naturally, this attitude puts you at a great disadvantage because you would have to change external forces in order to end your procrastination. Since external forces will continue to re-emerge, the battle goes on forever, and whatever ground you gain one day, you lose the next.

As the battle to gain external control proceeds unabated, the internal battle can relentlessly continue.

As an internalizer, you contribute to your procrastination problem by expending your energies in "thinking the problem out" in lieu of taking action. Your mind meanders around the topic of your weakness and why you can't overcome this problem. You blame yourself because you know what you "*should* do" and observe that you are not doing it. You see yourself as out of control and feel helpless—and so you procrastinate.

When you adopt a neutralizer attitude, you see your procrastination problem as being of no consequence and therefore make no attempt to directly overcome it. You adopt, in other words, a passive attitude. You exempt yourself from responsibility. Although this form of faulty thinking provides a sense of well-being, this sense is false and is likely to crumble at any time, leaving you vulnerable to intense feelings of anxiety.

# RECOGNIZING EXTREMIST THINKING PATTERNS

With patient effort you can develop skill in identifying and dealing with your own extremist thinking patterns that lead to immobilization or milder forms of procrastination. Admittedly, it is not easy to recognize such thinking, but the following guidelines can help:

- Be alert for what the general semanticists term *allness thinking*. Allness thinking is over-generalized thinking that takes the form of self-statements such as: "*Everybody* thinks I'm a failure"; "I *always* alienate others"; "You *never* show me any respect"; and "I can *never* do anything right." What this form of thinking represents is a sweeping indictment of yourself and/or others. Such extremist thinking is correctable by translating the statement into its specifics. For example, the statement "Everybody thinks I'm a failure" may readily translate to "John said I acted poorly when I delayed submitting my recommendations for improving the company's public image." With the problem translated and made more concrete, the problem is more easily dealt with.

- Be alert for absolutist statements like those including the terms *should*, *ought*, or *must*. While sometimes these words are neutral, more often they are highly evaluative words that signal a faulty evaluation. For example, you may believe that people should treat you fairly. Unfortunately, there is no law that reads that others should treat you according to your concept of fairness.

- Be alert for what I call disguised demands. Here the absolutist statements like *should*, *ought*, and *must* are in sheep's garb. Consider, for example, a simple question such as "I don't understand why I act that way." This *could* reflect a genuine question that could lead to constructive self-exploration. But such questions are often accompanied by anger or anxiety and can be readily and accurately translated into a statement such as "What a stupid idiot I am."

- Beware the label. Both Alfred Korzypski and George Kelly have noted that when people assume a label, they tend to act like the label. For example, a person who labels himself emotionally disturbed tends to act emotionally disturbed. It is therefore important to recognize the label as a form of overgeneralized or allness thinking and strive to eliminate it by stating problems in concrete or operational terms.

- Watch for the "is" (or "am") of identity in statements like "I am lazy," "He is a rat," or "I am a hopeless mess." This form of referencing is faulty, like most overgeneralizations, because the referent implies that the person *is* only one way and *is* condemned evermore to remain that way. Also, there *is* no way out of the label if the label *is* accepted as a fact. When you translate the "is" of identity to a concrete action, then you've taken some fuzz out of your thinking. For example, instead of "He is a rat," the translation could be: "I don't like Ralph's telling Bill that I am crooked." Once the issue is translated, you are at a better vantage point in determining if and how you will deal with the problem.

- Be prepared to complete allness statements. The allness statement "I'm no good" is incomplete because the reasons aren't spelled out. The simple addition of the word *because* and the reasons that follow help to complete the statement. With a completed statement, the criterion for worthlessness can be objectively scrutinized: "I'm no good" becomes "I'm no good because Jill said she did not want me to be one of her friends." Now the completed statement is more accurate and accessible to a fair evaluation.

- Watch for the rhetorical question. A rhetorical question such as "Wouldn't it be better if I didn't procrastinate?" leads to a monosyllabic "Yes," which has at best a neutral impact, and at worst a semantic guilt feeling attached. It is wiser to ask yourself questions like: "What do I procrastinate over?" and "What can I do to get it done?" which can lead to solutions.

- Watch for the "Have you stopped beating your wife?" type of self-question. You make yourself guilty before you can start to change. Some examples of this line of questioning are: "When was the last time I did anything right?" or "Why did I act so grossly?" These are guilt-trip–type questions that can send you down the proverbial mind tunnel toward grief.

- Be alert for vague abstractions like *meaningless*, *terrible*, *bad*, *no good*, and *awesome*. They clutter the mind and confound the thinking process. Make these words more concrete and you will be better able to see the problem you are disguising.

- Be alert for the indefinite referent *it*. Unspecified, the term *it* can represent verbal vagueness or fuzzy thinking. To illustrate: A client once told me that her mother was trying to force her to marry a man she disliked. Her statement was "I can't stand it anymore." What couldn't she stand? The mother's persuasive attempts? Actually, we finally determined that "it" referred to her feeling of tension and her fear of expressing her real feelings to her mother. When she translated the "it," the problem soon became manageable. Indefinite pronouns such as *everybody*, *nobody*, *they*, and *them* pose similar referencing problems comparable to the referent *it*.

- Try to identify mental contradictions. For example, many who procrastinate believe that they want to get their work done and believe that getting the work done should be easy. But when they don't get their work done, is it because they don't want to (although they say they do), or is it because getting it done is not so easy? At least one of the premises is clearly false. Another example is the person who believes he's strong yet acts weakly when it comes to following through on commitments. How can he be both strong and weak at the same time?

- Examine your thoughts and actions for cues that indicate you may be using external, internal, or neutralizing defenses. Specifically, watch for circumstances in which you blame others ("They/he are/is to blame for my troubles"), blame yourself ("I can't do anything correctly; what a jerk I am"), or act indifferently to important matters. Rather than blame or neutralize, concentrate on alternative evaluations that can be legitimately used to develop a fair perspective.

Now that you have guidelines, you are in a position to effectively use the following two exercises:

- Next time you procrastinate, tape-record your reasons and then play back the recording as soon as you have finished. Listen carefully for mañana, contingency mañana, and Catch-22 ploys, as well as for vague referents, abstractions, and overgeneralizations. As you are listening, pretend you are J. Thursday, defense attorney. Separate the facts from the inferences and fictions. (Remember, facts reflect concrete realities, such as: Oil floats on water; anything else is an opinion or inference.) Now, sticking to the facts, translate what you know into an action plan. For example—Fact: I have delayed two hours in returning my employer's phone call. Action: I will now return the phone call. (Notice, in the fact-action sequence, the absence of evaluative terminology.)

- Next time you feel anxious, angry, or depressed, tape-record your reasons. For the next half-hour, busy yourself with some alternative activity such as reading a newspaper. At the end of that time, play back the tape recording of your statement. Pretending you are Joe Friday, police detective, separate the facts from the inferences and fictions. (If you don't have a tape recorder, a written statement of your thoughts will do.)

Below I describe a rational-emotive system that you can use as a framework for using the concepts in this section. I will show how this method can be used to effectively deal with feelings of anxiety that lead to putting off.

# CHANGING FAULTY PREMISES
# USING THE ABC METHOD

Suppose you were handicapping yourself because you adhered to a fated-to-fail outlook like the one mentioned at the end of Chapter 7. "Fated to fail" is an attitude that whatever you undertake will turn out poorly. You don't really fear failure—you accept failure as a fact of life. Although you are willing to go through the start-up phases of an operation, you "fizzle out" in the stretch because you figure you are going to fail anyway. Such fated-to-fail attitudes are often effectively combatted by applying rational–emotive ABC techniques.

The ABC technique has been pioneered and developed by Albert Ellis. According to Ellis's method, $A$ represents an Activating Event, $B$ the Belief about that event, and $C$ the Emotional Consequence. Here is how the system works in combatting the fated-to-fail attitude. Suppose the activating event (A) is the opportunity to operate a frozen-yogurt shop, and the thought of opening the shop (B) leads to anxiety (C).

Suppose you believe (B) you are fated to fail. As a consequence of adhering to this idea, you passively go through the paces of opening the shop, but do so in a slipshod manner. After all, you think (B) you will surely fail in the long run (because you believe yourself to be totally inadequate). To summarize these data, you feel anxious, work halfheartedly, and believe you are going to fail eventually.

How, you may wonder, would Ellis tell you to proceed to deal with this fated-to-fail outlook? In Ellis's system, the emphasis is upon disputing erroneous beliefs that lead to crippling emotions and self-defeating actions. He uses a modified Socratic method to achieve his objectives, and here is how the method works.

The first step is to learn to identify and question false assumptions. You then learn to dispute erroneous ideas you may be maintaining (B). In other words, trace down the ideas and check them out (sometimes called reality testing). Thus the ABC system becomes the ABC$D$ system.

In employing the D phase of the system, you become a scientific defense attorney and ask penetrating and probing questions such as: How can I be absolutely sure I will fail in my yogurt venture? What will halfhearted attempts at succeeding as a yogurt entrepreneur lead to? How can I be totally inadequate as a person?

Realistic answers to these sorts of questions help develop a more accurate and objective outlook concerning the problem. Conscientiously answering these questions promotes the possibility of your developing that objective outlook and, with the new outlook, a fair perspective on your problem.

The ABC system can be employed in other situations in which you feel anxious and procrastinate. According to Ellis, people who experience anxiety tend to "catastrophize." *Catastrophizing* is a term he uses to describe the particular form of erroneous or faulty thinking that leads to feelings of anxiety. Very often this catastrophic thinking takes one or more of the following forms: "Wouldn't it be awful if . . .?"; What if . . .?"; and so forth. This catastrophic thinking develops when you perceive yourself as helpless or inadequate. Thus you anticipate disasters and see yourself as incapable of coping with these monsters you've created in your mind. Let's see how the ABC model can be employed to contend with this form of anxiety.

Your attack on the catastrophizing problem begins with asking and answering questions such as "Where is the evidence that the doom I am prophesying will actually happen?" Secondly, after assessing the probability (not the possibility, as *anything* is possible), look for proof that you won't be able to cope, even if some of your worst premonitions actually occurred. If you are having a hard time seeing how you could cope, pretend someone offered you $100,000 to invent five alternative strategies you could employ if worse came to worst and something happened like your losing your job (if that is what you were catastrophizing about). Chances are that under the $100,000 condition (or some other similarly highly motivating circumstance), you could be very inventive in identifying alternative coping strategies.

Suppose you believe you would be a worthless person if you

failed to cope effectively or acted helplessly in your fantasy of the catastrophic happening. Try asking yourself whether your best friend, if he or she were in your shoes and coped poorly, would forevermore be an unworthy person in your eyes and doomed for all time to live with this label.

With practice, these self-questioning techniques can bring to light many false conclusions and can help in a process of developing a realistic perspective.

## USING ATTRIBUTION THEORY TO CLEAR YOUR THOUGHTS

*Attribution theory*, growing out of the work of Franz Heider and George Kelly, states that a human perceiver attempts to understand action by finding a reason or attribution for the action. For example, if a drunk swore at you, you might feel mildly annoyed or find the incident humorous. However, if a sober acquaintance swore at you, you'd probably be inclined to regard the action from a different vantage point. The expletives uttered by the drunk and by your sober acquaintance may be the same, but the impact would differ depending upon the explanation (attribution) made about each incident.

Your explanation (attribution) to yourself concerning the actions of others is important, as it will tend to determine your actions toward those others. This is also true of the explanations (attributions) you give yourself concerning your actions. If, for example, you explain your procrastination as due to your being a lazy person, you'd be inclined to continue to procrastinate because you'd believe it's in your nature to procrastinate (you are an inherently lazy person). On the other hand, if you saw your procrastination as a consequence of faulty thinking and poorly developed work habits, then you might strive to change.

An important step in this process of change is to be objective in your self-explanation (self-attribution). Try to think scientifically, and this will aid your objectivity. By thinking scientifically, you couch your explanations in the form of hypotheses, and then you go about trying to disprove the hypotheses. For example, you hypothesize that all oranges taste the same. To test your hypothesis, you eat an unripened and an overripened orange and let your sense of taste validate or invalidate the hypothesis. Thus if you define yourself as "lazy," define *laziness* for yourself, and with this definition in mind, look for incidents to prove the exception. Now you can begin to make different attributions concerning your behavior and begin to work on those specific actions that you desire to change.

## REVERSING THE LABEL

Campbell's soup is not the same as the label, and if you think otherwise, try eating the label. Now, this statement may sound silly, but it is no more foolish than other statements in which the label is mistaken for the real object.

Labels, such as "It is *hard*," are affixed to certain types of work and experiences, and such labels can be the opposite of what the situation is really like. For example, maybe you put off making out your check to pay the monthly rent because it seems hard to do at the moment. Actually, the task is *easy*. Not mailing the check is harder because you still have the task to complete, plus you may be bothered by the landlord for being late. Such an added burden adds difficulty to the task. Thus, what appears harder is often easier, and what appears easier harder.

Various schools of psychotherapy talk about risk taking. The concept of *risk taking* simply means doing something risky that can be helpful in overcoming a problem. Actually, what is typically a better and probably more accurate way of saying the same thing involves substituting the concept *opening opportunities for risk taking*. Would you prefer to take a risk or create an opportunity for yourself?

Jumping into the 72° lake water for a swim can be defined as a cold and unpleasant experience or as cool and refreshing. How you label the experience determines how you feel about the experience.

*Valueless* is a label many affix to themselves to represent their whole being. Not only is the label *valueless* vague, abstract, and objectively meaningless, but the opposite, *valuable*, is inevitably more accurate.

If you practice flipping labels upside down (reversing them), you can open opportunities for yourself to think more flexibly. Try label-flipping, using the following terms as a start:

- out of control
- weak
- incapable
- thoughtless
- clinging
- carefree
- happy
- worthwhile
- sensitive

Is it possible that at any one time you could only be one of the above labels or its reverse?

# 10

# Your Imagination Can Help You Get It Done

"In the world of dreams, anything is possible."

You can use your imagination to trigger positive action to overcome procrastination. Through the use of imagery, you can create a mental picture to help you overcome this problem. Before we proceed, however, try to see if you can produce mental pictures. Practice creating a mental image of a watermelon, ripe and oozing with sweet juices. Can you see the picture in your mind's eye? Is the color vivid? Can you almost taste the fruit? Perhaps your mouth is watering. If so, you are pretty good at creating mental images.

Some people are not very good at creating pictorial images. Maybe you are somebody who has trouble, or cannot create such images. If you fit into this category, then obtain a sketchpad and some colored felt-tipped pens or watercolors. Use this material to draw the images. As you draw or paint, try to get into the feelings these pictures create. Don't worry if your drawing efforts won't win an art award. Your purpose is to create an atmosphere or effect for yourself. Even if you can only draw stick figures, if those stick figures help you to create an atmosphere, you are accomplishing the purpose of this exercise.

In this chapter I am presenting word stimuli for mental images to help create an antiprocrastination outlook. These stimuli have helped people overcome resistance to getting it done. As you read these examples, try closing your eyes, imagining those images, and thinking about the stories or questions accompanying them. Focus particularly on those images that might simulate situations that apply to your own special brand of procrastination problem.

Through imagination, you can loosen defenses that normally interfere with your getting it done. Thus the more real and emotive you make the image, the more likely you are to gain a sharp experiential awareness of the nature of your procrastination problem and insight into how to deal effectively with it.

I will present nine situations. Try to imagine the situations I describe. Contemplate the situations and let your reactions tell you if this system of creating constructive mental events can aid you in getting it done. But before you begin, find a comfortable spot where you are likely to be free from interruption for the next several hours so that you can be free to use your imagination.

## THE TIGER AND THE PUSSYCAT

Are you afraid of the unknown? Does this dread spread to other activities that you see others fearlessly doing? If so, do you put off embarking upon doing something new if the territory is unfamiliar? Do you believe there is danger to your self-image if you are not immediately expert in a new field? Do you immobilize yourself because of these preoccupations? If the answer to any one of these questions is yes, then the first imaginary journey can help you to develop an alternative perspective.

Pretend you are walking through a lush, green jungle in a foreign land. You have lost your way and you are hungry and tired when you finally arrive at the base of a tall stone wall. You hear very faint sounds on the other side of the wall—a sort of rumbling or purring sound. Hark—is it the sound of a tiger or the sound of a pussycat purring in the sun? Are there people behind the wall? Are they friendly and will they help you, or will they seize and imprison you? What will these people be like—tigers or pussycats?

When you put off learning something new in a territory unknown to you, what is the terror you create in your mind? When you fear the unknown, there must be something within that causes you to frighten yourself—what is it that you really fear?

## WHAT DOES YOUR ANXIETY LOOK LIKE?

Each of us feels anxious from time to time. When you feel anxious, you generally concentrate on how you feel. What would happen if, instead, you tried to imagine what your anxiety looks like?

Imagine giving your anxiety a form. Perhaps even draw a picture of what it looks like. Does your anxiety take a humanoid or an animal shape? If it's humanoid, dress it up in a little Lord

Fauntleroy outfit and place a red- and gold-striped beanie with a pinwheel on its head.

Do you still take your anxiety so seriously? Once you have imagined how your anxiety appears dressed up in silly garb, think of a task you are putting off because you feel anxious. Imagine the task and imagine that silly anxiety is trying to stop you by frightening you.

## MAKING OIL AND WATER MIX

Do you think you can make your life wonderful by getting your friends and family to do things your way? Have you chanced to notice that the more you push them to change, the more resistant they become?

For you, the great converter, the following image has special merit. Imagine yourself trying to blend Quaker State Motor Oil and crystal-clear water from the Quabin Reservoir in Massachusetts. You've decided that you want to stop light oil from floating on the top of your crystal-clear water, so you devise a technique to drive it down to the bottom. To accomplish this feat, you obtain a trough of Quabin water, a gallon of oil, and a large wooden paddle. You proceed by pouring the oil on the top of the water and begin vigorously to slam it down with the paddle. Imagine yourself working hard at this task, and imagine the oil bubbles floating leisurely back to the surface, as they are naturally inclined to do. Now you slap all the more vigorously, thrashing and slapping the oil and water together.

After you've rested from engaging in this tiresome fantasy, try to imagine the person you would most like to change (other than yourself), so that he acts exactly as you want him to act, and imagine what it is like to continually and directly change this person to match the way you want him to be.

## WHAT WOULD YOU DO IF YOU WERE SOMEONE ELSE?

We all have fantasies of what we could do if we were different from what we are. Certainly, if you were the ideal you, you would act in many ways differently from the way you currently do. Imagine what that ideal would really be like. (Would you be like someone else? Or like an improved version of yourself?) What would you be doing with your life that is different from what you are currently doing? What would your interpersonal relationships be like? What type of work would you be doing to earn a living? What type of hobbies would you enjoy? Would you travel? If so, to where and how often? What would be . . . ?

## IMAGINE WHAT DOUBLE TROUBLE IS REALLY LIKE

Double trouble is when you have a problem, such as procrastination, and then depress, anger, or worry yourself into procrastinating more or worrying more about how bad you feel. In using imagery to combat this problem, first try to imagine yourself running through a well-worn country pathway and arriving at the start of a long road heavily layered with green, warm grease. Imagine yourself walking along this long, slippery roadway, wanting to get to the end quickly. Now pretend that you are running fast to get to the other end of that road as soon as possible. Imagine your feet pounding harder against that oozy grease. Imagine how the harder you run, the more you slip and fall, plastering your body with that warm, gooey grease! Can you see the subtle messages of this image as clearly as you can the obvious?

## IF I WERE A PRIVILEGED CHARACTER

The fantasies we have considered so far are designed to help counter procrastination. Some of your images, as has been implied throughout this book, help foster putting it off, and they need to be exposed and countered. One such image is that of the privileged character who deserves continual eleventh-hour reprieves when he procrastinates. If you put yourself into this mold, to counter this self-defeating fantasy imagine the president of the United States deciding to grant you the special privilege of being able to put off whatever you wanted for as long as you wanted without having to pay the consequences (not that he actually has the power to do this). You would never have to concern yourself with acting responsibly again. Now imagine the president pleading your case before a joint session of Congress, begging that you should have repeated extensions on everything, including paying your taxes, so that you should never have to suffer the pangs of feeling bad for putting things off. Congress grants this request and proposes that your case be put before the world leaders so that wherever you travel in the world, you will have immunity from responsibility. In a special series of meetings the president makes major military and economic concessions and finally secures agreement from this esteemed body to put the issue to a vote before the world population. Imagine people pouring out of straw huts, country mansions, and midtown apartments to vote on whether to grant such a universal privilege. And when the vote is counted, it's unanimously agreed that you should have endless reprieves. You are now voted a nonprocrastinator through the goodness of the people of the world. You have now a unique privilege: the official right to act irresponsibly.

The above exaggeration can be embellished, so as your imagination carries you to greater heights of exaggeration, periodically pause and reflect upon the meaning of the eleventh-hour reprieve.

## THE GETTING-IT-DONE TRIP

Suppose you had a unique opportunity to be superefficient for one week—would you take the opportunity? Here is the situation: Imagine that a magic genie that you've released from imprisonment in an old cola bottle has granted you a week during which you would be able to accomplish all that is humanly possible within that time. Here is how the deal works—you have an hour to identify what you want to accomplish during that week. For the rest of the week, aside from sleeping, you will be in a state of complete command over your desires and actions. In this state, you will be able to move effortlessly from one project or desire to the next. As you progress, you will use your time effectively to get your projects done right.

During your week of maximum efficiency, your efforts will be coordinated and you will not be detoured by the usual diversions. In effect, your actions will be realistic and your timing excellent. In other words, you will not suffer the disillusionment so many suffer when their minds seize upon opportunities their abilities can't equal.

What would you like to see yourself getting done during this week-long period of efficiency and effectiveness that the genie has granted?

Let your mind wander with this fantasy as you sit on your favorite spot. Be the realistic person you are capable of being on this fantasy trip of yours.


## MAÑANA CONFRONTS TODAY

Pretend you are Mañana, the Great Tomorrow, waiting with clenched fists to take what will have been needlessly put off by Today.

Today has lots of confidence in you, Mañana, but you suspect that despite Today's glorification of your capabilities—and how flattering that glorification is!—you will still have something nasty to say to Today for passing on to you what you do not want to do.

So there you are, the great Mañana, anticipating being piled under the remnants of Today. Knowing what is in the offing for you, you decide to try to change the course of your history. You unclench your fists and decide instead that you will not blame Today. Rather, you will try to rehabilitate Today. You recognize that you want Today to do a favor for the self Today will become tomorrow (you), so like a tolerant and helpful teacher, you lend aid and support and knowledge. You do this because you recognize that when the Great Mañana becomes the Great Today, there will

be much to do that is new and necessary without having to contend with the debris from the past.

So entertain this zany fantasy where you are both Mañana and Today. Carry on a dialogue with yourself for approximately fifteen minutes in which both Mañana and Today work out their mutual getting-it-done problem to mutual satisfaction.

## SING A MERRY TUNE

Imagine yourself a concert singer on the stage with the national TV cameras focused upon you as you are about to sing the song on the following pages as an introduction to an ensemble about the art of procrastinating.

Whenever you think of putting things off, think of this song and let your natural spirit of determination do the rest.

# Procrastination

130

**MARCH TEMPO**

CE·LE·BRATE. YOU'LL CE·LE·BRATE. YOU'LL PUT IT OFF AND LET IT WAIT. AC-

CU·MU·LATE, AC·CU·MU·LATE, FAL·LING BE·HIND IS A NAP·PY STATE. IT'S

SUCH A JOY. THE PER·FECT PLOY WAST·ING TIME IS THE ONLY WAY PRO·CRAS·TI-

NA·TION. PRO·CRAS·TI·NA·TION. PRO·CRAS·TI-

NA·TION. TO·DAY MA-

**SOUTH AM. FEEL**

ÑA·NA MA·ÑA·NA SO A·ME·RI·CA·NA SO MUCH TIME TO BOR·ROW,

JUST DO IT TO·MOR·ROW MA·ÑA·NA MA·ÑA·NA,

SO A·ME·RI·CA·NA SO MUCH TIME TO BOR·ROW JUST DO IT TO·MOR·ROW

PRO·CRAS·TI·NA·TION PRO·CRAS·TI·NA·TION PRO·CRAS·TI·NA·TION.

# FANTASIES CAN COME TRUE

When you fantasize, you become emotionally and intellectually involved in a pleasant or unpleasant, exciting or relaxing, imaginary experience. Furthermore, there are no limits to the types of fantasies you can experience.

Among the many varieties of fantasy, there is one that bears special consideration: productive fantasy. Many scientists, poets, and inventors find inspiration for some of their most important creations in their imagination. Some fantasies have been anticipatory of inventions to come. Jules Verne's *20,000 Leagues Under the Sea* illustrates how a fantasy preceded the development of the submarine.

Even though you may never develop or anticipate the development of inventions or works of art through fantasy (of course, you might), this power of yours for productive imagination can be harnessed by converting your good ideas into action. How is this to be done, you wonder? Use your imagination.

# 11

# Getting
# in Touch
# with
# Your Feelings

"Feelings, feelings—what is life without feelings?"

Each of the following descriptions can evoke a feeling. See what feeling they evoke in you.

- A deep-red rose shrouded in green.
- A large, dark, rapidly advancing beast.
- An old man with eyes half-shaded.
- The command "Do it or you are fired!"

- Soaking in a warm bath.
- A fifty-dollar bill lying lonely in the grass.

Feelings are pleasant or unpleasant. Feelings have meaning and have direction. Feelings come in many varieties: sadness, contentment, happiness, hate, concern, love, excitement, peacefulness, anger, boredom, jealousy, warmth, fright, care, trust. Some feelings tend to be simple (warmth). Some feelings tend to be more complicated (lassitude). Feelings are sometimes mixed: love and hate, anger and joy. Positive feelings seem less complicated (liking). Negative feelings sometimes seem more complicated (depression).

People sometimes fear certain of their feelings and seek to insulate themselves from all feelings. Some people are so dominated by their intellect that their minds neutralize their feelings. They are overly analytical and often mentally diversionary, and rarely speak of feelings. This dominance is exemplified by the "INTELLECT–FEELINGS" diagram.

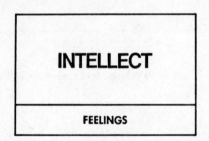

Some people feel driven by their emotions and experience themselves as if they were rudderless ships foundering in everchoppy waters. These are the folks who are likely to focus upon their feelings and not on their thinking (see the "FEELINGS–INTELLECT" diagram).

People who routinely have trouble getting it done and who procrastinate typically exhibit a failure to harmoniously integrate a balance between their thoughts and feelings, a balance exemplified by the "INTELLECT←→FEELINGS" diagram.

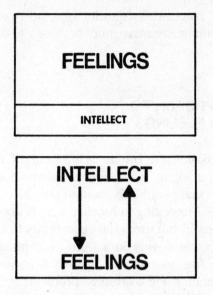

When overemphasis is upon either feelings or intellect, the net effect is a restriction of the range of feeling and creative ideas and a slowdown in the flow of actions.

It has been my observation that the more one tends to procrastinate, the more one tends to be rigidly closed to one's positive abilities and feelings. Paradoxically, however, the more closed to experience, the more sensitive one tends to be.

This last statement requires explanation. People who become involved in all sorts of mental, emotional, and behavioral entanglements often do so because they are afraid of their own "soft sensitivities": They tend to be fearful of being tender, showing love, expressing annoyance, admitting or showing vulnerability, expressing concern or self-doubts, and admitting what they really want. These sensitivities are often covered by a façade of toughness promoted by a fear of being overwhelmed or controlled if such sensitive feelings are exposed.

The toughness is really weakness. And this presumed toughness reflects a form of maladjusted sensitivity: sensitivity to self-image, sensitivity to painful emotions, sensitivity to loss of control, sensitivity to being taken advantage of. And this is the paradox—

the harder one runs from exposing genuine strengths (soft sensitivities), the more sensitive one becomes to threats to one's cover.

## ROGERS' APPROACH TO CONTACTING FEELINGS

Carl Rogers pioneered the development of client-centered psychotherapy, a highly positive-constructive counseling system that emphasizes that people have within themselves the capacity to help themselves. According to Rogers, what is necessary to release these capabilities for full use is the opportunity to explore the inner reaches of one's personality in a warm, accepting atmosphere in which one can feel free to call upon his resources to mentally expand opportunities and to resolve problems.

A major emphasis in Rogers' approach is an emphasis upon the counselor's empathetically helping his client to sort out feelings and to gain clarity concerning desires and wishes. To accomplish this objective, the counselor listens receptively to what the client says and then skillfully reconstructs and reflects what the client is trying to say. In this fashion, the counselor acts like a mirror so the client can more clearly see himself. This reflective–reconstructive process aids the process of recognition and articulation of feelings, as the following therapy episode recorded between one of my clients and me reveals:

Jane: My daughter-in-law, Sue, has been pretty rude to me lately. She hasn't called and didn't send a thank-you note for the birthday gift I sent her. When I think of her rudeness, I get shaky inside, kind of nervous. Sometimes I feel like screaming at her.

Bill: Sounds like you are feeling very angry with Sue.

Jane: Yes, I feel angry. I don't think she should be treating me the way she does. Yes, I do feel angry with her. . . . But, I know she has been having trouble on her job lately. . . .

Perhaps she has been too preoccupied. She used to be more conscientious.

Bill: You seem to feel angry with Sue, but you also seem to be saying you feel confused about her motives for not keeping in contact with you—she doesn't seem to be acting like herself.

Jane: Yes, I guess I was feeling pretty angry with her, but now that I am talking about my feelings, it's strange that I do not feel so angry anymore. I sort of thought I was nervous at first, but I really was angry. I didn't want to admit that feeling to myself. I also think I was concentrating so much upon myself that I forgot about Sue's job problems.

In this short period of time, Jane became more aware of her underlying feelings of anger. She showed acceptance of this feeling by acknowledging the feeling and not blaming herself for feeling as she did. Furthermore, she was able to quickly put herself into her daughter-in-law's shoes in an attempt to understand Sue's problem.

Carl Rogers talks about the importance of *openness to experience*. By this he means a willingness to acknowledge and accept one's being. Openness to experience also means an awareness and acceptance of personal feelings and attitudes. When one is open to experience, one is better able to see life as it is. One has, in fact, a realistic awareness of oneself in the present moment.

People who act on the basis of a simple, uncomplicated understanding of themselves and of their experiences are better able to acknowledge and articulate the obvious and say how they feel. Such congruent, constructive self-expression can be quite profound.

But there are many ways in which reality can be twisted, complexities invented, and profoundness lost. We have already discussed how this happens: self-doubting, discomfort-dodging attitudes leading to diversions, happiness contingencies, and various other mental entanglements. These entanglements all represent faulty awareness or blocks to the sort of awareness that emanates from an openness to experience.

## MAKING CONTACT WITH FEELINGS

Openness to experience can be increased by practicing using feeling words to accurately describe your inner reactions. The following list compares feeling-word expressions with nonfeeling-word expressions and so may serve as a model for practicing such expressions:

| Feeling-Word Expressions | Nonfeeling-Word Expressions |
| --- | --- |
| I felt annoyed when I saw you throwing your shirt on the floor. (Annoyance) | Don't throw your shirt on the floor again. (Annoyance) |
| When you said you appreciated my help, I felt warm and good all over. (Appreciated) | Glad to help out. (Appreciated) |
| I really feel quite bland about this year's political election. (Neutral, indifferent) | This election isn't worth thinking about. (Neutral, indifferent) |
| I felt good laughing at that comic. He had some really funny lines. (Happy) | The comic was funny. (Happy) |
| I felt really disappointed when you did not return my phone call. (Disappointment) | How come you didn't call me back? (Disappointment) |

Note that feeling-word expressions lend greater clarity to your meaning, as they include clear referents to your feelings. Some of the nonfeeling-word expressions tend to be ambiguous, so when clear, unambiguous communication is necessary, the feeling-word-type expression may be a more accurate way of communicating.

Putting yourself into your experiences (expressions) is an extension of the feeling-word expression. This method is also helpful as a way of heightening your awareness of your inner feelings. Like the feeling-word exercise, putting yourself into your experiences can make your communications more colorful, accurate, and vivid. The following illustrates a neutral description style and a style of putting yourself into your experiences:

*Situation:* Going to the zoo to see a panda.

*Neutral description:* I went to the zoo to see a panda. After I saw the panda, I walked around the grounds and looked at the other animals.

*Putting yourself into your experience:* I felt very desirous to see the zoo's new panda. So I eagerly went to the zoo. And. when I saw the great panda, I felt a rushing sense of excitement. To me, the animal was beautiful and graceful, and I felt so absorbed in watching his funny antics that I watched him for hours. Later, with an uplifting feeling of delight, I meandered about, visited the other animals, and threw peanuts to them.

Putting yourself into your experiences can be practiced in writing (as in the above), or by picking a solitary place and talking aloud to yourself about what you have just experienced, or in a brief vignette uttered to a friend.

In putting yourself into your experiences, it is often better to avoid the use of superlatives, such as "marvelous" or "wonderful," unless you really feel marvelous or wonderful. Superlatives are often trite baggage.

Incidentally, your feelings need not be powerful before you express them. Sometimes expressing a "low-level" feeling can make the feeling come more meaningful and alive. Nor must you make putting yourself into your experiences your only style of communicating. If you did, its effectiveness, like that of any overused tool, would wear down. However, periodic practice with this method can help you become more sensitive to your own soft sensitivities.

## PERLS'S PILLOW TALK

Rogers' reflective counseling is helpful in clarifying real feelings and promoting openness to experience. Among other methods, Fritz Perls's gestalt-therapy methods are helpful in identifying underlying feelings in those cases in which such feelings may be carefully concealed or misunderstood.

Perls's popular pillow-talk technique often proves effective in evoking real feelings and their conceptual foundations. The following case from my psychotherapy files represents an adaptation of Perls's method and is presented to illustrate my version of the pillow-talk procedure. You might find this method helpful to adopt for your own use in identifying troublesome impediments to getting it done.

Lynn's sleep had been interrupted for seven consecutive nights because of a recurring and frightening dream of a "missing thing." She spoke about her problem during group therapy, and when neither I nor the group seemed to be able to help her clarify what was really bothering her through conventional methods, I tried the pillow-talk approach.

Lynn's job was to talk to a pillow. Her first job was to speak to the pillow from the frame of reference of the "missing thing" and to allow herself to say whatever came to mind without censoring herself. She began by saying, "I am the missing thing and I will visit you every night. I will keep you awake and you won't be able to control me. I will haunt your nights."

Since the word *control* seemed to be a key word, I asked Lynn to speak to the pillow as if she were a mental entity called Control. She began by saying to the pillow, "I am Control. You are afraid of me because you can't channel me. I am too elusive for you to manage. I am out of your grasp, but I still command you."

Since the key concept in this sequence was fear (the word *afraid*), Lynn played Fear in the next pillow-talk episode: "I am Fear, and you are too inadequate to deal with me. I am too powerful for weak little you to control. Your missing thing is strength to deal with me. I am all-powerful."

In a brief discussion that followed, Lynn admitted that she felt very inadequate and had numerous self-doubts. She thought there was something wrong or missing within her that rendered her ineffective in dealing with life.

As a last step in this pillow-talk sequence, we decided that the pillow would now represent Fear, and that Lynn would be herself and challenge this fear of hers, using Albert Ellis's ABC technique. In her monologue with Fear, she was encouraged to present her strengths to challenge the claim that she was inadequate and that she was missing the ability to cope. She actively engaged in this dialogue for the next twenty minutes, and as the dialogue progressed she began to sound firmer and more confident. Nearing the end of the pillow talk, she asserted that her missing potential had been found.

The next week Lynn reported to the group that her "bad dream" occurred no more. Furthermore, she gave examples of taking action—strong command over her actions—as she asserted herself in developing a long-put-off résumé, followed through on a long-promised dinner party for some of her friends, and asked her upstairs neighbor out for a date (a secret wish she had had for many months).

The pillow-talk episode helped Lynn to help herself get in touch with her inner fears and inadequacy feelings; the episode provided her with an opportunity to overtly express her strengths. The way was paved to untwist the lies she had been telling herself about how frightened and inadequate she was. Unblocked, she began to take solid steps toward change—she began to do what she had been putting off.

## BRINGING UP THE FEELINGS

Carry on pillow-talk conversations with yourself in the following areas:

- Pretend you are Procrastination talking to yourself. Spend five minutes being Procrastination and talk to yourself as represented by a pillow. For the following five minutes, make the pillow be Procrastination and challenge what Procrastination had to say to you.

Repeat the same exercise with:

- self-doubt
- discomfort dodging
- fear
- perfection
- control
- approval

At the end of this exercise, jot down in your log what you have learned about your feelings and about yourself as a result of this exercise. Plan how will you use this knowledge in your self-improvement program.


## USING YOUR ACTIONS AS CUES
## TO YOUR FEELINGS

Your actions can be cues to your feelings. For example, if you ask for advice and then counter suggestions with statements preceded by "Yes, but . . .," what are you saying about how you feel? If you dress slovenly and walk slumped over, what does your appearance tell you about how you are feeling? These are but a few cues that can help you to better identify what you think and feel about yourself.

The following exercise is designed to evoke feelings that correspond to certain actions. Look over the list of actions, and if you notice some that you engage in, try to identify the underlying feelings:

| Action | Feeling(s) |
|---|---|
| helping a good friend with his or her project | _____ |
| spending time with interesting people | _____ |
| playing to win | _____ |
| dressing sharply | _____ |
| cheating at cards | _____ |
| working diligently | _____ |
| manipulating a friend | _____ |
| saying what you mean | _____ |
| starting false rumors | _____ |
| walking the dog | _____ |
| blaming people for their faults | _____ |
| repeatedly showing up late | _____ |
| holding back expressing feelings | _____ |
| delegating authority | _____ |
| buying a gift | _____ |
| washing the dishes | _____ |
| studying mathematics | _____ |
| walking on the other side of the street when you see someone you know | _____ |
| maintaining a sloppy apartment | _____ |
| straightening up whatever is out of place | _____ |
| following through on disliked projects | _____ |
| eating an ice cream cone | _____ |
| looking for a new job | _____ |
| starting a family | _____ |
| playing catch | _____ |

# 12

# Getting Yourself Organized and Following Through

"People who have a sense of well-being have one common characteristic—they are organized, mentally and behaviorally organized."

The benefits of using an effective organizational system are extensive. Perhaps if you can see the phenomenal advantage of developing such a system and using it conscientiously, you too will be able to rid yourself of the sort of disorganization that results in procrastination.

Improving your organizational abilities can have a constructive double effect. You'll be able to effectively deal with what needs doing and you'll be building up confidence in yourself as a person who can confront and handle organizing problems of many types. Specifically, developing and using an effective organizing system has three solid advantages:

- Personal maintenance and administrative functions will be completed in an efficient, orderly fashion.
- Anxiety over misplaced materials and over living and/or working in a cluttered, disarrayed environment will be diminished.
- Time freed from needless replication of effort and worry can be better used organizing and chaneling efforts toward goals of self-development and fulfillment.

Developing this most effective personal organizing system is no mean feat! Corporations spend fortunes to develop their internal-control systems and prize such systems as being among their most valued proprietary possessions.

## HOW TO GET ORGANIZED

There are many types of organizing systems. The best, however, reflect a four-step process:

- identifying organizing objectives
- determining how efforts can be directed to increase efficiency and effectiveness in meeting organizing objectives
- developing the system
- revising and/or updating the system

Obviously, the system needs to be detailed and the various elements coordinated. The development of the system can be not only a thoughtful but also a creative endeavor, one that you can ultimately take a sense of pride in.

Good organization can result in rewards that go beyond creative satisfaction. By being better organized, you may gain as much as the equivalent of a year or two of time (perhaps even more!) during the course of your life to be used for more creativity, productivity, and pleasure. For example, if your system saves you just fifteen minutes per day from rummaging for misplaced items or frustrating yourself by obsessively ruminating over what to start first, you will gain the equivalent of almost twelve eight-hour work days each year.

There are many ways to avoid frustrating yourself, wasting time, and simultaneously make more efficient use of your time. Some basic hints on organizing that can help you gain more time include some of the following:

- Identify your priorities and work on them in preference to other, less important and/or difficult projects.
- Continually review your priorities and modify them as new circumstances warrant.
- Set time aside when you will not be disturbed as you work on your priorities.
- Maintain adequate and up-to-date records.
- Establish a workable filing system and use it.
- Tackle new work as soon as possible.
- Set aside time each day for dealing with the unexpected.
- Try to get some of tomorrow's work completed today.

These eight hints, in conjunction with the four-step organizing process, merely represent the outline of a good organizing system. Here is a potpourri of general organizational hints that you can include as part of your organizational system:

- When the mail arrives, immediately rid yourself of obvious junk mail (unless you like to read junk mail).
- Set aside a time each day or each week for completing correspondence.

- Set aside a time each day to check on your progress so as to keep yourself well directed or on target with your plans.
- Make use of mechanical organizers such as "in" and "out" boxes, card files, and schedule books.
- Use a message board for attaching notes about tasks that are important to complete.
- When a short phone call can substitute for a letter, use the phone.
- Delegate responsibility whenever possible.
- When working on especially important projects, find a place where you are not likely to be found or disturbed.
- Organize books in your library alphabetically or by subject matter so you can find the ones you want quickly.
- Plan vacations well in advance.
- Note important dates like birthdays on a calendar that you refer to daily.
- Set specific times aside to do recurring chores.
- Pick a task a day as your designated task. If you complete it, consider your day a success.
- Keep important phone numbers where you have easy access to them.
- Keep your phone list updated.
- Try to be one week ahead on at least one project.
- Avoid overscheduling yourself.
- Routinely throw out old clothing and articles for which you have little use.
- Keep only items you regularly use on shelves.
- Do a task when you think of doing it.
- Take along reading materials on buses, trains, and airplanes.
- Make arrangements for a friendly grocer to take phone orders and deliver groceries.
- Order gifts and other retail items by catalogue.

- Live as close to work as possible to cut time in transit.
- Purchase gifts well in advance of needed occasions (during routine shopping trips).

This list naturally consists of *time-saving strategies* that can be used singly or in combination. Some of the suggestions may not be applicable in your case, but others will. You also can compile a list of time-saving strategies, perhaps an even more extensive one. Keep in mind that the purpose of developing this time-saving system is to give you more hassle-free time for doing what you want to do.

How about follow-through? Once you have devised your plan, there are many strategies you can use to get yourself started and maintain your momentum. Let's consider some helpful aids for following through.

## PRACTICAL STRATEGIES FOR FOLLOWING THROUGH

There are virtually thousands of methods you can use to assist yourself in following through on implementing your organizational system. Since it is desirable to avoid procrastinating on your organizational system, I will spell out some helpful methods that I have recommended for many years and described in an article, "Overcoming Procrastination," in 1973.

### The Five-Minute Plan

When you consider starting a project, it is sometimes difficult to move from this contemplation phase into action. Your reluctance may be due to your view of the whole project as burdensome and overwhelming. The answer to this problem is the *five-minute plan*. In employing the five-minute plan, you commit yourself to begin and to work on the task for only five minutes. You commence action, and at the end of this time period you decide if you will continue for the next five minutes. At the end of that five-minute interval you again decide if you will continue. You work the five-minute system until you decide to stop or the task is completed.

There is nothing magical about an interval of five minutes. Indeed, you may prefer an interval of ten minutes in order not to interrupt yourself so frequently. One caution: If you decide on time periods over fifteen minutes, you may be reluctant to start. Fifteen minutes may seem too long. Experiment with the method until you find an interval ideally suited to your temperament.

The principles underlying this strategy are:

1. It is easier to begin a task if you initially commit yourself only to short, successive work intervals.

2. Once you have initiated an action, it tends to gain momentum "by itself" until you get tired, are interrupted, or the task is completed.

3. There will be a positive striving to continue with the task, once initiated, because each step brings you closer to completion.

## Bits-and-Pieces Approach

Have you ever allowed tasks to pile up to the point where you thought you'd be smothered by them? You look around and see that you have dishes piled up, newspapers scattered, and you can't see where the dust leaves off and the furniture starts. When viewing this frightening sight, you have a sense of being overwhelmed, and you are confused as to where to begin.

When you arrive at this state of confusion and can't decide upon your priorities, it doesn't matter where you start, as long as you start. A sensible technique to use under such conditions is the *bits-and-pieces technique*. The bits-and-pieces technique involves arbitrarily selecting any one of the tasks. Once the task has been selected, immediately start whittling down this first task, and when this task is completed, progress to the next and continue until you have completed what had previously overwhelmed you.

Using the bits-and-pieces approach does not require you to set a deadline. Instead, you work on the selected task(s) as long as you are able. Then you resume the project, if only for a few minutes, at your next available opportunity. Using this method, chances are you will not complete the huge mound of work in one magnificent expenditure of energy, but you will begin to see progress. (Incidentally, with practice, the bits-and-pieces approach can develop into a constructive habit.)

## Reminding Yourself

During any one day, you may be bombarded with many distractions that sidetrack you from mailing a letter, making a phone call, purchasing that needed box of laundry detergent. If you try to make mental notes, you'll probably forget some of the details, as the inevitable distractions keep disrupting mental reminders. You need, therefore, to insure yourself against forgetting.

Doing the task when you think of doing it is one solution. Making a list is a second. But it is not always possible to implement action or to make a list at the instant you think about it. For example, you may be riding on a bus and remember that you have an important call to make. Even though you can't make the call right away, you can make a written reminder to yourself in a notebook that you carry specifically for that purpose. Placing notes in your wallet may also help—every time you make a purchase or receive cash, you will see the reminder. Conscientiously using this system, you reduce your chances of a delay that is due to memory lapses.

A reminder system, useful as it may be for normal lapses of memory, can be even more helpful for reminding yourself to deal with a procrastination problem. There are several ways in which this system can be adapted. One very helpful method is to make up reminder cards and place them in strategic positions. The cards list a specific task or tasks that you'd like to complete, such as writing a letter to a friend. Place each card in a prominent position so that you'll be sure to see it.

A second technique involves using a symbol to signify a task that you routinely wish to accomplish. For example, suppose you select a green dot to symbolize exercising. You could place a small round piece of masking tape on the center of your watch and color it green. The idea is that whenever you saw the dot—and that would probably be frequently—you would be reminded that you want to exercise daily.

A third method involves writing self-reminding phrases on a card. One of my favorites is "Doing It Gets It Done." Naturally, you should prominently display this card. One of my clients found a good spot for hers. She taped it to the ceiling above her bed. It was the first thing she saw upon awakening. What she did when she saw the card was to begin the day by doing something positive to combat and alleviate her procrastination problem. This reminder system, as you can imagine, has many variations and uses. Try a few and see if you can't find one that works.

## MORE FOLLOW-THROUGH STRATEGIES

If you have a busy daily schedule filled with administrative tasks and responsibilities, it's easy to put off the more mundane ones. You may put off these tasks because they are dull and uninteresting, but you may also get distracted and legitimately forget them. One method you can use to assist yourself in remembering to start getting these tasks done is the *cross-out-sheet system.*

The cross-out-sheet system is a simple method that merely involves making a list of activities that are important to complete that day. You work on the items in their listed order. As soon as you complete an item, you cross it off. Then you immediately move on to the next item and begin to work on it. This rapid shift from one activity to the next is important because it allows you to use the momentum generated by your previous effort.

The list need not be used just for daily entries. You can have a separate list for weekly tasks, or one consisting of items representing your long-term goals. With these weekly or long-term lists, cross out each item as completed before you move to the next. Crossing out provides you with a rewarding sense of pleasure, since it represents an accomplishment.

The cross-out list is a versatile, easily modified technique. You can, for example, list the items in their order of priority. Or you can use an alternating sequence, listing items you are likely to put off and those that are less burdensome or more pleasant, then combining the lists by alternating these items. Chances are that if you follow this sequence, you are more likely to complete all the items on the combined list because you'll be motivated to rid yourself of an unwanted detail in order to move on to a more interesting item. (See Chapter 13 for a description of the Premack principle, which provides the theory for alternating items.)

The *set-go* technique can be an effective aid in overcoming procrastination. Like the cross-out sheet, it has many possible variations.

Many people do a fine job in their preliminary organizing, like getting out paper and pencil to write a letter, buying detergent to wash the dishes, or gathering basic research to write a report. Once these materials are assembled, however, attention is turned to other matters and consequently one falls behind on the work that was once so carefully organized. Part of the reason for putting off following through is often that one gets a feeling of accomplishment from just having *set up* to start the task. So the problem is not in the *set* part of the set-go sequence, but in the *go* phase. The following are some ideas to help with the *go* part:

- Imagine yourself setting up your work and without pausing beginning work to complete it. Keep the image in mind as you actually set-go with a task.

- Use a paradoxical technique in which you tell yourself that it is absolutely impossible for you to set up a task and then go on directly to complete it. Be as convincing as you can as you set up to go. (Paradoxical tactics sometimes work because of a tendency many people have to rebel against the commanding statement "You can't do it.")

- Announce in writing to your family and friends that you are going to overcome your set-go problem by both setting up and going right away. (This sometimes works because many people find it hard to back away from doing something they have willingly publicly committed themselves to do.)

- After you have set up a task, pull your earlobe three times, then start. (Pulling your earlobe, or some such activity, is an interruption in the regular habit sequence of setting up and putting off. Thus, as a disrupter, it makes it easier to refocus on going.)

There are many more ways to aid the follow-through process once you are organized, and so in the next chapter we turn to behavioral methods you can use to assist in this process.

# Following Through by Rewarding Yourself

"Getting it done is my reward."

Previously I have discussed how to become better organized. In this chapter I will discuss a framework for understanding and employing behavioral strategies to help you to follow through on your organizational or developmental plans. This approach to reducing procrastination uses behavioral aids based upon reinforcement principles that are powerful psychological tools that you can use to add clout to your antiprocrastination program.

Behavioral and reinforcement techniques have a long and

controversial history. Unfortunately, the general public has often greatly misunderstood these techniques. Part of the responsibility for this misunderstanding originated at the door of John Watson, the father of behaviorism, who around 1913 claimed that, using behavioral techniques, he could make a doctor, lawyer, or chieftain out of any child. Despite his claim, as history has shown, he never succeeded, and neither has anyone else. Sensationalism surrounding behavioral techniques has continued periodically with exaggerated accounts of its dangers. Science-fiction films like *A Clockwork Orange* have also added to the mystique of behavioral methodology.

The methodology described in this chapter derives from the work of the psychologists Edward Thorndike, B. F. Skinner, and other psychologists who have built upon Thorndike's and Skinner's work to develop and employ reinforcement techniques in helping people develop and maintain control of their lives. These psychologists and psychotherapists include Thomas Coates, Alan Kazden, Michael Mahoney, Donald Meichenbaum, and Carl Thorensen, who have refined and applied these methods to help people cope with their psychological–behavioral problems.

## SELF-CONTROL METHODS

Psychological hedonism, a concept derived from the nineteenth-century motivational doctrine of Jeremy Bentham, is based upon the idea that pleasure assures its own recurrence by rewarding the actions leading to it. So we tend to direct our actions to secure rewards and to avoid unpleasantness. These rewards or *reinforcements* can be levied by yourself or by others. Some of the methods behavioral scientists have developed to help you use rewards effectively rely upon your own capacity for self-regulation.

There are many rewarding self-initiated follow-through actions you can use to help yourself. In order for these techniques to work, however, it is important for you to make a firm commitment to conscientiously use these methods until you have reached your goal.

Before proceeding to consider strategies, it is important to first examine what is generally meant by rewards and punishments.

## REWARDS

Rewards are used to *increase* the frequency of an activity. They come in two varieties: positive and negative. You can use both types to improve your performance in order to consistently get done what you normally procrastinate on doing.

Positive rewards add pleasure or benefit and follow action. For example, if I scratched my head and a ten-dollar bill fell into my lap, you'd probably witness me scratching my head again and again as long as the ten-dollar bills continued to fall. This is because getting ten-dollar bills for scratching my head is rewarding to me. I will continue in this and other activities as long as they are rewarded.

The concept of negative reward or reinforcement works on the same principle as positive reward. The basic difference, however, is that you get your reward by *ending* something that is unpleasant. Stating your opinion, for example, may be reinforcing if it marks the termination of anxiety about stating that opinion.

## PUNISHMENTS

As rewards come in two general varieties, so do punishments: positive and negative. Punishments are used to *decrease* the frequency of an activity.

When you use positive punishment procedures, you *act to avoid losing some pleasant activity or object*. You do your homework, for example, so that you will be allowed to watch your favorite TV show. In other words, you try to decrease the time you spend avoiding homework. And to put teeth into this endeavor, if you fail to do this homework, you are deprived of the experience of watching the show.

When you use negative punishment procedures, on the other hand, you complete an activity so as to *avoid experiencing pain*. You do your homework, for example, so that you can avoid the painful mental experience of failure. You avoid touching a hot stove to avoid feeling the sharp pain of a burn. Snapping your finger hard against your cheek every time you are *tempted* to smoke a cigarette is another form of negative punishment, one that can be used to suppress the urge to smoke: You avoid smoking to avoid the painful snap.

Punishment may not always work to suppress a particular behavior. For instance, if you wanted to teach your child to stop insulting you and you invoked a penalty from time to time when he uttered an insult, you still may not be able to stop his insults. For example, the child may learn through trial and error to make the discrimination that if he insults you while you are busy cooking or talking on the phone, you will not punish him. Thus, the child may curb his insults in some instances but not in others. Unless you are able to deliver an appropriate punishment systematically each time the child utters an insult, you may not be able to stop his insults.

Rewards, on the other hand, have a better rate of effectiveness. If, for example, you rewarded your child with something that he really likes each time that, under the conditions he is apt to make an insult, he instead said something pleasant, it is more likely that the reinforcement will substantially reduce or stop the insult-making behavior. Even if you fail to reward him each and every time he is noninsulting, he is likely to continue to work toward achieving the reward by not making insults. In fact, not knowing whether the reward will come may provide him with an incentive to work even harder to obtain the infrequent rewards.

Rewards and punishments can be administered by other persons or by you. The administration of these rewards, however, can be haphazard. Thus, in developing a self-control program to overcome procrastination, it is important that you design a program that you can carry out in a systematic fashion.

In using self-control strategies it is also important to proceed in a step-by-step fashion, tackling one procrastination problem at a time. Just like any other habit, the procrastination habit is usually overpracticed and thus quite difficult to break. Thus, if you proceed by tackling one problem at a time and obtaining the inherent rewards of your success, you are more likely to succeed overall.

## DESIGNING YOUR SELF-CONTROL PROGRAM

The first step in designing your self-control program involves *defining the specific procrastination problem* that you want to alter. At this stage it is very important to limit the definition to one that is specific, clear, and behavioral. You want to be clear with yourself, and you don't want to bite off more than you can chew and end up overwhelmed by the project. The idea is to concentrate your efforts on improving your antiprocrastination skills so that you will have maximal chances of succeeding. This success can then serve as an encouraging experience that can help stimulate you to tackle another, and possibly even tougher, procrastination problem.

It is important to formulate your goal in behavioral terms— that is, in the form of actions that you wish to either increase or to decrease. Using such behavioral terms will aid you in two ways: First, it will make levying rewards and punishments much more clear-cut, and secondly, you will be better able to decide whether you have succeeded in achieving your goal. If you use vague, non-behavioral language, on the other hand, you will probably be less able to decide when to reward yourself and when you have succeeded. An example of a vague goal is "to become effective." Some examples of specific behavioral goals include: to increase daily studying behavior by three hours, to decrease television watching between the hours of 6:00 and 11:00 P.M., and to decrease weight by ten pounds.

Once you have described what you wish to accomplish in terms of a behavioral goal, you may begin the next step— *pinpointing the times or conditions in which you are going to initiate your program*. For example, you decide you want to increase your daily studying time by three hours and begin by surveying your studying behaviors. You find that you have several hours each morning that you could use for study purposes. Thus, you establish that your program will be conducted in the morning, and you specify your behavioral objective: to study for college courses three hours each morning, Monday through Friday, between the hours of 7:00 and 11:00 A.M.

The next step is to *break up the goal into small sequential steps* that lead gradually to goal attainment. It is important to make the first step something that you are likely to do, and to build gradually from the first to the second and the third and fourth (and maybe more). By making the steps small you increase the likelihood that you will succeed at each step and thus reap the reward and the incentive to continue. You might, for example, start with a small amount of time performing the goal-oriented behavior (studying) and then gradually increase the amount of time. Or, more practically speaking, you might break down the program into steps and follow each step with a reinforcement. The table is an example of a self-control study program using the step concept:

## SELF-CONTROL PROGRAM FOR INCREASING TIME IN STUDYING

| Goal | Objective | Steps | Reinforcements |
|------|-----------|-------|----------------|
| To increase time in study by fifteen hours per week. | Study at desk in living room between the hours of 7:00 and 11:00 A.M. Monday through Friday | Night before set alarm clock for 6:45 A.M. and place materials to be used for studying on the living room desk. | Can watch 11:00 P.M. news after alarm is set and materials laid out |
| | | Arise when alarm rings in A.M. | Can wash face and brush teeth. |
| | | Begin studying at 7:00 until 8:00 A.M. | Can have breakfast between 8:00 and 8:30 A.M. and read the newspaper. |

| Goal | Objective | Steps | Reinforcements |
|------|-----------|-------|----------------|
| | | Return to studying 8:30–9:30 A.M. | Can listen to half-hour of music on stereo at 9:30 A.M. |
| | | Return to studying 10:00–11:00 A.M. | Can read comic book at 11:00 A.M. |
| | | For each 5 consecutive days of studying according to the above schedule | Option: <br> • Seeing movie <br> • Going out to eat <br> • Watching baseball game <br> • Playing tennis |

The fourth step in the formulation of your self-control, anti-procrastination program involves the *identification and implementation of rewards and/or punishments*. As explained earlier, rewards are generally more effective than punishments, so it would be most advantageous to use rewards rather than punishments. When identifying rewards, it is important to set a reward that is desirable for you to obtain. Your self-control program will not work unless your rewards are worth performing for. These rewards must be something desirable enough so that you feel motivated to do something that you usually put off, so think carefully and come up with rewards that you are certain to want. In addition to rewarding yourself at the end of the project, rewards can follow each sequential step (as in the program above). Each time you complete a step in your program, you deliver an appropriate reward to yourself. Thus, the rewards should fit the behavior that you have just completed—the best type of reward is one that you can give yourself right after you successfully complete each step so that you know you are getting that reward for each unit accomplished. In addition, you may add bigger rewards as you progress in your program. You might, for example, reward yourself by treating yourself to a movie after five consecutive days of studying. Your rewards will vary with your individual taste and desires, but it is essential that you only reward yourself *right after and not before* completing each step.

In deciding on appropriate rewards you may wish to use David Premack's principle. Premack's principle is that any actions that a person engages in frequently (high-probability behaviors) can serve as rewards to increase infrequent behaviors (low-probability behaviors). Using the Premack principle as a source of reward is highly beneficial because such high-probability behaviors are usually readily available and can be used immediately after a certain action takes place. To indentify such high-probability behaviors, go through the day and think of the things that you enjoy doing each and every day. Perhaps such activities would include: taking a shower, combing your hair, drinking a cup of coffee or tea, or reading the newspaper. To use these as rewards you simply make one of these high-probability behaviors contingent upon the completion of one of your sequential steps to goal achievement. Thus, for example, if you succeed in studying from 7:00 until 8:00 A.M., you can take half an hour out and have breakfast, drink a cup of coffee, or read a newspaper. If, however, you do not successfully complete the chosen step, you do none of the above that morning.

Another reward system that you might find useful in your self-control program is that of the accumulation of points. To use this system effectively, you give yourself a point and write it down on some type of scoresheet immediately after you succeed in completing a step. This method of reward allows you to reward yourself immediately by providing yourself with a symbol that visually displays your accomplishment. Naturally, if this visual display is not rewarding, don't use it.

As suggested above, punishment can also be used in your self-control program: You can agree with yourself that if you fail to meet your objectives, you will penalize yourself. Types of penalties that you can use in your self-control program include: depriving yourself of something that you very much desire; wearing a heavy rubber band on your wrist and snapping yourself with it after each negative behavior begins; forcing yourself to do something you dislike very much, such as writing and mailing a very positive letter of praise to someone you dislike.

Punishment may also be used in combination with reward. You select a behavior that you wish to get rid of, punish yourself when you engage in it, and systematically reward an alternative, positive behavior. You might, for example, find that you spend too much time watching TV and avoiding study, so you set your behavioral goal: to eliminate TV watching and to increase studying between the hours of 7:00 and 11:00 A.M. Then you proceed to set up sequential steps that lead to a reduction in TV watching and lead to a concomitant increase in studying. You penalize yourself each time you watch TV between 7:00 and 11:00 A.M. while you reward yourself each time you make one of your sequential steps. This type of combination reward-punishment approach is usually quite effective if the rewards are delivered soon after the positive behavior and if the penalties are consistently enacted immediately after you start to engage in the unwanted activities. Punishments will be effective only if you levy them consistently, following each time you fail to achieve an objective.

The final step in your self-control, antiprocrastination program involves *stabilization of the behavioral change*. After you have been successful with your program, it is important not to discontinue reinforcement right away. To ensure the continuance of change, it is best to continue to reinforce yourself for positive behaviors. As a means of stabilizing the positive behavior, it is better to use a system of *fixed-interval reinforcement*. What this means is that instead of rewarding yourself each time you engage in a positive behavior, you reward yourself only after a fixed time period when you have succeeded in attaining your goal during that set period of time. After succeeding in studying from 7:00 to 11:00 A.M. for five days, for example, you might give yourself a special reward by going to a movie you've been looking forward to seeing. You do this for several weeks, giving yourself a reward each time that you successfully study for the five-day cycle. Then you begin to gradually increase the length of time between rewards. For the next few weeks, for instance, you might only reward yourself after ten days of successful studying as prescribed by your self-control goal and use a different reward, such as purchasing a long-wanted sweater. As you continue to succeed in carrying out your goal and receive rewards further and further apart, you gain practice in this new positive habit that you have developed. Eventually, your new, nonprocrastination habit will become firmly implanted in your schedule of everyday activities.

As an aid in increasing your knowledge of self-control methods so that you can continue to improve your ability in getting it done, I will give additional examples of how you can use rewards and punishments in developing your self-control program. (Some of the learning principles already cited are presented to help stabilize your knowledge of them.)

## REWARD SYSTEM— VARIABLE TIME LIMIT

The *reward system with a variable time limit* is used to overcome procrastination problems in which there is no clear deadline and it is thus difficult to predict when a task can be completed. Such problems include: losing weight, completing the first draft of a book, or learning the basics of a foreign language.

In developing a self-control program when the task does not have a defined time limit, you first set up a specific goal, using the conditions that usually result in your procrastinating to make the goal more specific. Suppose, for example, that you've been procrastinating on losing weight. After taking a hard look at what usually happens each time you try to lose weight, you realize that you frequently go out for dinner either alone or with friends, and you overeat. Under these circumstances, you might set up your self-control program with the following behavioral goal: to lose twenty pounds and neither make nor accept dinner dates until your goal is accomplished (naturally you'll eat moderately at that dinner). Next, you select a suitable reward that you believe to be commensurate with your efforts. With this procedure you set no deadline to finish your program. Meeting your goal may take weeks, months, or years. However long it does take, you don't get the reward until you complete the antiprocrastination task. Also, you can't lose the reward unless you don't complete the goal. Therefore, it is just a matter of time until you succeed in getting your just due. Thus, if this reward is something that you really value, you'll work all the harder to attain it.

One very important point to keep in mind when choosing your reward is to avoid rewards that could be counterproductive. For instance, if you are trying to lose that twenty pounds and finally succeed, it would be counterproductive to "reward" yourself by ordering and then eating a large piece of cheesecake when you go out for dinner.

## REWARD SYSTEM— FIXED TIME LIMIT

This model is designed for use in procrastination situations in which there is a deadline that is important for you to meet. Such deadline situations may include personal maintenance goals, like paying bills, or personal development goals, like applying before the deadline for graduate-school admission. You find that you typically procrastinate on this sort of goal and consequently get dunned by your creditors or block your own progress by delaying your education.

In order to combat procrastination and meet your deadline, you first assess the extent to which you procrastinate, the conditions under which you procrastinate, and what you can do to increase your getting-it-done activities. After surveying your particular situation, you may find that you procrastinate a little or a lot. You may, for example, pay some of your bills on time, or you may not pay any of your bills on time. Next, you look at the conditions under which you are most likely to procrastinate. You may find, for instance, that you are most likely to procrastinate on paying your bills at the end of the month because you haven't budgeted your money and don't have enough money to pay them at the end of the month. You may decide at this point that you could end your procrastination problem if you put $150.00 aside from each paycheck to be used exclusively for paying recurring bills, like the one for rent.

With such deadlines, it is normally unnecessary to set up small, sequential steps, since paying bills and applying to graduate school are not long-term endeavors, and the time spent setting up sequential steps might better be used working to complete your goal. (In working with many people who procrastinate, I have found that setting up sequential steps sometimes becomes a burden, hindering the actual accomplishment of the antiprocrastination task). Thus, you may find it helpful to experiment with some programs using a sequential-step approach and other programs in which you levy a reward at the completion of the total program when sequential steps are not specified.

So, when you are experimenting by not specifying sequential steps, you identify your behavioral goal, and you proceed directly to the formulation of rewards for your success. These rewards may include: eating a piece of apple pie, watching a favorite TV show, calling a friend, taking a walk, reading the newspaper or a favorite magazine, taking a hot shower. Whatever you decide to use for your reward, it is most important to make your reward reasonable. Say, for example, that your antiprocrastination goal is to spend an hour formulating a budget. You wouldn't want to reward yourself by taking a week-long vacation or by watching four hours of television. Clearly, the reward would be too high. Also, you might end up using that reward as a means of further procrastination on other activities. Thus, it is essential to set rewards that are commensurate with the amount of effort that you put into attaining your goal.

## POSITIVE-PUNISHMENT TECHNIQUES FOR MEETING DEADLINES

Positive-punishment techniques can be used effectively when there is a *deadline* for completing the goal. This deadline may be self-imposed (in cases where you are able to set a reasonable deadline for yourself), or the deadline may be externally imposed.

Either way, you set up the specific behavioral goal and then select an appropriate penalty for yourself that you or someone else dispenses if you don't accomplish your goal. In many cases, it will be better to seek the aid of a friend to dispense the punishment. If you know that the punishment will *really* be carried out if the job is not completed within the specified deadline, you are more likely to work to meet the deadline. Whatever you decide would be an appropriate punishment, it is essential that the punishment be worse than the procrastination "consequence" (not completing the task on time). Only if the punishment is something that is very unpleasant and only if you realize that this punishment will be carried out if you don't get the job done will you really exert an effort to stop procrastinating.

Let's see how this method works. Let's suppose that to date you have not written your new job résumé and your current job is due to end within the month. Naturally, you want to motivate yourself to stop procrastinating, start writing the new résumé, and commencing job hunting. You decide to use a positive-punishment technique to help yourself.

Now, let's suppose that your favorite movie, *King Kong*, is coming to television and that you are super-eager to watch it. So you decide to arrange the contingencies for yourself such that if you do not have the résumé completed and professionally typed before the movie, you won't watch *King Kong*. Indeed, to assure the success of this operation, you enlist the aid of a friend who promises to remove a tube from your television set or rip the cord from its socket and snip the plug just before *King Kong* comes on the air if you don't succeed in completing the résumé before that deadline.

## NEGATIVE-PUNISHMENT TECHNIQUES FOR MEETING DEADLINES

When you use positive-punishment procedures, you work to avoid losing something that is pleasurable. With negative punishment, on the other hand, you inflict something negative upon yourself if you fail to live up to your pledge to overcome procrastinating on a particular task. As with positive punishment, you want the punishment to be more severely unpleasant than procrastinating. Let's suppose, for example, that you have been procrastinating on buying your spouse a birthday gift. If you don't buy it on time for the celebration, your spouse will act angry and upset. You have decided you want to buy the gift on time, and this year you have decided to use negative punishment to get it done. You agree with yourself that you will penalize yourself if you fail to purchase a gift before the birthday celebration: You decide you'll wear a smelly fish head around your neck commencing one week prior to your spouse's birthday if you haven't purchased a gift by that time. Furthermore, you'll continue to wear the fish head in plain view until you've bought that gift.

If the fish-head punishment is a bit too radical for you, you could also use a penalty like ordering food you dislike at a restaurant and slowly eating it. Other punishments you can include in your list are letting the air out of all four of your own automobile tires, or smashing your watch. If you choose your consequence well, you'll *avoid* the pain by achieving the goal on time.

Like positive punishment, negative punishment techniques are helpful with goals that have a deadline, and it is important that the punishment be inflicted if you don't reach your deadline.

## SPECIAL TACTIC: ALTERNATION TECHNIQUE

The alternation technique is a method I have developed and found quite effective. Let's see whom this system will be helpful to.

Suppose that you are a person who overeats, smokes excessively, and chews gum and wants to quit all three habits. For years you have been overweight, hacking and coughing, and running up dental bills for dislodged fillings and new cavities. You'd like to eliminate all of these health hazards, but not at the same time. To do this, you set up a system of eliminating each one by one by "playing" one against the other.

This is how this system, the *alternation technique*, works. First you set a goal for how much you want to weigh and a new eating program that involves eating only certain foods in clearly defined quantities. Every day that you exceed the quota you have established for yourself, stop smoking and chewing gum for the next twenty-four hours, commencing at the exact moment you exceed your food quota. Continue with that program until you achieve your goal and have maintained your new desired weight for six weeks. Next, develop a program to enable you to stop smoking. First decide the maximum number of cigarettes that you will allow yourself to smoke per day. (Let's hope this number will be zero!) For every day that you exceed your quota, you can't chew gum the following day. When you succeed in giving up smoking, begin working on giving up your gum-chewing habit. For your program to give up gum chewing, select another habit you wish to get rid of and "play" that against the gum chewing. Conscientiously applied, the alternation technique has several advantages. You are weakening the gum-chewing and smoking habit each time you evoke the penalty for having exceeded your food quota. If you rarely evoke the penalty because you are losing weight by consistently adhering to your plan and building confidence in your ability to constructively alter your eating habits, you have mastered an approach that enables you to systematically progress in the elimination of other unwanted habit patterns.

## CONTINGENCY CONTRACTING

The above self-monitoring techniques have the inherent problem of enforcement. If you don't systematically enforce them, they are of little value in aiding you to overcome your procrastination problem. To ensure such systematic enforcement, you can add another prop to increase the likelihood that you will comply. That extra prop is a written *contingency contract*, which involves another person to assist you in your antiprocrastination endeavor.

The process can be as simple as stating that you will do the laundry within two days or your friend will spend a five-dollar bill you have given him to hold for you. First write out a formal statement to this effect; then you and your friend sign the statement. Then turn the five-dollar bill and the contract over to your friend and collaborator. Naturally, this system is not foolproof. It won't work if you can talk the friend into giving back the money or if the loss of the five dollars isn't enough to make much difference to you. With contingency contracting it is of utmost importance to make the penalty worse than the "crime." It is also essential to spell out the activities that you intend to engage in, how and when you plan to engage in them, and, when possible, to provide a deadline for completion. Indeed, the more you are able to pin yourself down specifically and concretely, the more likely you will be able to complete the job. Vague promises to yourself in writing are virtually worthless. Promising to overcome procrastination, for example, is of little help unless you define the areas in which you procrastinate and define how you will proceed to work to change. So try to be clear in defining your problems and how you will approach them. You'll position yourself for greater progress if you do.

Self-monitoring or self-control techniques are helpful adjuncts to employ in stimulating yourself to follow through on tasks that you normally put off. These techniques are only effective if you make them effective. They can be made more effective by enlisting the aid of an ally to enforce a contingency contract. In all cases, the clearer and more concrete your self-control program or contingency contract, the simpler it will be to follow through with it.

# 14

# Three Strategies for Ending Procrastination

"A good structure helps one keep on target."

In this chapter I will describe three strategies you can employ to deal with your procrastination problem. They are *action planning*, *charting*, and *action pattern analysis*. Each is an antiprocrastination tool you can use to free your time so that you have more time for more enjoyable living. As an addendum to this chapter, a case description is provided to illustrate how a procrastination pattern can evolve out of a single incident.

# ACTION PLANNING

Have you ever heard the expression "think ahead"? This saying means: Consider your future and plan for it. Thinking ahead can be as implicit, simple, and informal as deciding to continue to work ten more years in the civil service so that you can collect retirement benefits. At the opposite extreme, a plan can be as explicit, formal, and complicated as a five-year corporation plan emphasizing growth through acquisition of smaller industries. Whether your plans are simple or complex, formal or informal, implicit or explicit, they are highly important in providing guidelines for your future.

Without well-conceived guidelines, you rely on wishes and hopes to rule your destiny. By waiting for opportunity to knock, you place yourself in a passive role: You take what life has to dish out and therefore end up settling for whatever crumbs happen to fall your way. Worse yet, when you routinely procrastinate, you are apt to let many of the better crumbs (opportunities) slip by. Without planning ways to accomplish what you set out to do, your energies will tend to be dispersed. By planning ahead, you heighten your chances of selecting the good fruits rather than settling for the remnants.

You don't have to be an expert in action planning to make plans. Some simple guidelines will suffice to provide you with the necessary tools:

- Identify your goals.

- Spell out the conditions that will make the attainment of your goals worthwhile (criteria for satisfaction).

- Define the intermediate objectives or steps leading to the attainment of your goals.

- Identify the procedures that will help you to move toward attainment of your goals.

The explicit steps in this sequence provide an orderly progression of thought and action leading to the attainment of your goal. The model can be adapted to any area in which you tend to procrastinate, including locating a new home, selecting a new job, or rising to the head position in a corporation.

To enable you to better visualize this type of planning process, I will briefly present an example, a case from my psychotherapy files. A client was procrastinating getting a new job. His company was permanently shutting down, which necessitated that he find a new job. Two of the reasons for his procrastination were his indecisiveness concerning the type of work that he was equipped to do and his indecisiveness regarding what he might enjoy doing. His goals (step 1), therefore, were to identify what he *could do* and what he would *like to do*. Because he had a master's degree in business administration and enjoyed management jobs, he decided to confine his search to the industrial area, with the aim of working in a management capacity. With this overall goal defined, he moved to step 2 and tried to define the working conditions most likely to promote greatest satisfaction. As it turned out, this proved to be the most difficult, yet most fruitful, phase. In thinking the problem through, he determined that for him to be happy in a job, his work would have to provide him with opportunities for:

- identifying problems hampering productivity
- designing solutions for such problems
- implementing actions following his planned solutions
- exposure to a wide variety of problems within his specialty area
- working for a solid, growth company
- opportunities for advancement and recognition

This phase proved most fruitful because it clarified what he wanted from his work. This information made it easier for him to define objectives or steps leading to the attainment of his goal. He defined these steps as:

- preparing a résumé describing his background
- drafting a letter outlining his job objectives
- practicing effective approaches to present himself in interviews
- locating, through personal contacts and library research, companies likely to be interested in him in the capacity in which he would like to work because he had the skills to help them solve their problems
- making contacts with companies in which he would like to work

The final step involved planning and designing strategies to implement his objectives. For example, in developing his résumé, he obtained samples of other well-written résumés, read several books on résumé writing, drafted a model résumé, asked for comments from knowledgeable friends, revised the résumé based upon good feedback, and had the finished product printed. He outlined the steps for implementing each of the other objectives and carried them out. In the end he was rewarded by finding the type of job that met *his* criteria.

You, too, can make and carry out a plan to get what you want. In this process making a written plan will probably serve you best because written plans will better enable you to directly assess the plan's feasibility and give you flexibility to sketch in modifications. The written plan, furthermore, reduces the chances that you will forget important details. Although this plan can be spelled out in sentences, my own preference is for an outline format. The outline is easier to revise, and the steps stand out. But you can judge for yourself. The table on the next page, "Action Planning," is the outline for selecting a new job that my client developed.

## DEALING WITH EMOTIONAL PROBLEMS

When you put off dealing with problems concerning your emotional health, you perpetuate your emotional stress, and as you continue to experience stress, you will often put off personal de-

# ACTION PLANNING: SECURING A NEW JOB

| Goal | Criteria for Job Satisfaction | Objectives | Procedures |
|---|---|---|---|
| To obtain a satisfying job in management | 1. Identifying problems | 1. Identify rapidly growing companies | 1. Companies |
| | 2. Designing solutions for identified problems | 2. Prepare effective methods of marketing self |    (a) Personal contacts |
| | 3. Implementing actions according to design | 3. Secure interview opportunities |    (b) Standard & Poor's stock reports |
| | 4. Variety in work | 4. Obtain job |    (c) University placement office |
| | 5. Work for solid growth company | |    (d) Private placement agencies |
| | 6. Opportunities for advancement | |    (e) Newspaper ads |
| | | |    (f) Personal knowledge |
| | | | 2. Marketing |
| | | |    (a) Professional résumé |
| | | |    (b) Cover letters, individualized for target corporations |
| | | |    (c) Placement agency assistance |
| | | | 3. Interviewing |
| | | |    (a) Follow-up on letters and agency referrals |
| | | |    (b) Simulated practice in interviewing |
| | | |    (c) Personal interview |

velopment goals because your energies become consumed by un-resolved problems.

This bound energy can be released and you can do this in a systematic fashion. The strategy you can use is called *charting your problem* and has been effective in helping many who previously put off dealing with emotional worries and troubles.

Using a charting technique, you can develop a clear map of your problems along with action-plan solutions to channel your energies the way you want them to flow. A simple charting procedure involves three major categories of activities:

- problem diagnosis
- defining advantages of change
- action planning

In the "problem diagnosis" step, you identify attitudes and/or fears that you *believe* motivate your particular procrastination problem. Your goal is to be both honest and specific with yourself in labeling what you believe to be self-defeating fears and attitudes. To achieve this result, introspect or discuss your problem with some-one who is not only objective but who can also help you pin down the problem to its basics. In this diagnostic endeavor, your purpose is to identify how you are currently perpetuating procrastination. (Avoid delving into your past for childhood causes at this point. The next section describes a method for recognizing patterns stemming from this period.)

The second step involves identifying the clear advantages of changing your procrastination pattern. (You do this to give yourself a positive incentive for change.) The third phase involves develop-ing specific action plans targeted toward reducing your procrastina-tion problem by increasing pro-efficiency actions. You make these plans concrete by specifying the exact activities you will perform to overcome the problem (*how-to* technique). This process will be experimental, and it will be helpful if you make revisions as you proceed. If you conscientiously follow the above procedure, the clarity you obtain and the changes you make doubtlessly will prove productive.

To illustrate this process, I have chosen a case in which the client's problem was punctuality. This client chronically arrived late for work and for appointments. She also delayed sending out reports and answering correspondence. As a consequence, her job was jeopardized. The table on pages 178 and 179, "Charting Your Problem," describes her problem diagnosis, advantages of change, and action plans. Incidentally, she worked her plan well and constructively changed.

## ACTION-PATTERN ANALYSIS

Most people are interested in learning the historical causes of their problems. If you wish to embark on a psychological expedition to examine your problems historically, an *action-pattern analysis* can be a helpful technique. In action-pattern analysis you are not interested in searching out the originating causes of your procrastination problem. Instead you:

- Focus on one procrastination problem you've felt plagued with for many years.
- Try to identify common elements in the repeated episodes.
- Examine each of these episodes in terms of trying to identify erroneous or distorted ideas and/or self-defeating actions (reality-testing phase).
- Consider alternate antiprocrastination actions you can take to change your circular pattern.
- Apply this knowledge as you actively work to change your procrastination-habit pattern.

To illustrate, let's suppose you are currently procrastinating writing a report for your company, and you want to try the action-pattern-analysis method to gain insight. You first concentrate on identifying past examples where you've procrastinated when you had a writing assignment. By tracing your problem, you recall that while in college you had a similar problem—putting off writing term papers until the last possible moment. In comparing these two examples, your analysis leads to the conclusion that there are two common elements in present and previous examples:

1. You think you are a poor writer and that your efforts are futile and will lead to failure.
2. You usually write in bed propped up by a pillow and quickly fall asleep.

In the next step (*reality-testing*), you examine the evidence for each of the two conclusions. The evidence for item 1 derives from the fact that your best English grade was a B-minus, criticisms that your writing is fuzzy, and criticisms that your writing includes numerous grammatical and spelling errors. Item 2 is supported strongly by the evidence that you do most of your writing in bed when you are able to take work home.

To obtain a fair and honest appraisal of your writing history, you also look for evidence to contradict your first two conclusions as a second part of the reality-testing. Contrary to your first conclusion, you have received praise for your writing of personal letters, essays on topics of interest, and descriptions of your own ideas and opinions. Furthermore, when you write letters, interesting essays, use your ideas and opinions, you sit at your desk.

By concentrating on illustrating your procrastination writing pattern with positive writing-experience examples, you gain a more concrete perspective on your writing problem. The assimilation of these data leads to an accommodation to them wherein your self-concept as a writer is modified to fit the evidence. The analysis further leads to an action plan that takes these data into account. You decide to write your report in a personal style, highlighting what is of particular interest to you and reflecting your own ideas and opinions. To assure the report will not be delayed because you fall asleep on the job, you write the report while sitting at your desk.

# CHARTING YOUR PROBLEM: LATENESS

| Diagnosis of Factors Contributing to Personal Ineffectiveness and Lateness | Advantages of Change |
|---|---|
| 1. Anger | 1. Relief from unnecessary tension |
| 2. Rebellion | 2. Avoid unnecessary hassles |
| 3. Helplessness (basis of items 1 and 2) | 3. Improve quality of interpersonal interactions |
| 4. Fear of: | 4. Better scheduling of time |
|    (a) People | 5. Increased time for creative and productive pursuits |
|    (b) Change | 6. Avoid getting fired from job |
|    (c) Expressing Anger | |
| 5. Habit | |
| 6. Need for control | |
| 7. Need for comfort | |
| 8. Self-doubt | |

## ACTION PLANS

| Anger and Rebellion | Fear | Discomfort | Self-Doubt |
|---|---|---|---|
| 1. Recognize basis of resentment<br>(a) Unfulfilled expectations<br>(b) Failure to be victorious, etc. | 1. Admit fear<br>2. Identify erroneous assumptions<br>3. Cope with anxious anticipations<br>4. Allow self to engage in problem-solving activities | 1. Allow self to experience uncomfortable feelings<br>2. Accept tension as part of living<br>3. Acknowledge feeling as signal for antiprocrastination action<br>4. Identify and fight against comfort-seeking tendencies | 1. Identify strengths<br>2. Express strengths in action<br>3. Recognize that action involves risks *and* . . .<br>4. There is no guarantee that action outcome will be successful, *but* . . .<br>5. Purposeful activities promote personal growth *and* . . .<br>6. The development of better coping skills, *and* . . .<br>7. Habit breaking |
| 2. Recognize underlying feeling of helplessness | | | |
| 3. Engage in purposeful action<br>(a) Be honest in self-expression<br>(b) Encourage others to express, themselves | | | |

## THE CASE OF A SINGLE
## PIVOTAL EVENT

Although historical analysis of a procrastination problem does not normally lead back to a single pivotal event, occasionally there is an exception. The following case illustrates such an exception, as it is important when attempting to unravel a problem, such as procrastination, to keep open all possible avenues to understanding the problem.

John was a bright, frightened, frustrated man of thirty-four. Since his graduation from high school, he skipped from one job to the next, rarely remaining for longer than a year and typically quitting within a month. He used his vocational instability as an excuse for avoiding relationships with women. Yet one of his strongest wishes was to marry and to raise a family. In striving to seek an answer for his unhappiness, John entered therapy.

During the course of therapy, John wanted to understand why he was repeating patterns of quitting jobs and avoiding relationships. The analysis of John's problem led to a simple explanation. As a result of his therapy, John was able to target in on one major episode in his life that was reflected in his current procrastination problem.

It seems that when John was eight years old he overheard a relative's comment on the appearance of his eight-year-old cousin Ralph. John remembered the relative saying that Ralph was a handsome child. He also recalled feeling anxious and depressed when he thought that he must be ugly since the relative made no favorable comment about his appearance. Thus he came to see himself as ugly.

John's belief that he was ugly was buttressed by two related false conclusions: Ugliness equals worthlessness, which equals undeservingness. This simple faulty concept served as a powerful procrastination-creating principle. No wonder John would not allow himself to progress! No wonder he procrastinated! He believed he was unworthy and undeserving of the good fruits of life.

John had twenty-six years of that faulty logic to reverse, and so his problems did not dissolve overnight. He had to learn to over-come a historically negative bias against himself and to begin to act according to a new concept of enlightened self-interest. His first step in this endeavor was to practice acting the way he would like to think and feel. That included approaching, dating, and following up contacts with women he found attractive. It also included getting training for the sort of vocation he secretly wanted—investment counseling.

Few procrastination problems can be traced to a single piv-otal incident. Although it can be argued that the "handsome child" incident merely served to kick up a problem lurking beneath the surface, such an interpretation in this case is trivial, because once John recognized his childhood perception as faulty, he found him-self motivated, after the insight, to change. And change he did! He worked hard at his problem, eventually found a great woman to marry, and is currently developing his career and enjoying his family.

# 15

# Putting It All Together

"The end ends at the beginning."

I trust that at this point in your reading you are feeling realistically optimistic about improving your ability to do it now. Realistic optimism is rewarded by changing faulty thinking and getting yourself into action, so in this chapter I will draw together many of the concepts described in this book as an aid to help you to organize your efforts so that you can put a comprehensive getting-it-done plan together.

The first part of this chapter presents materials to review and for extending your awareness of procrastination—its acquisition and maintenance. The second part of this chapter presents a structured step-by-step program to help you proceed in getting it done by showing how the material thus far presented can be integrated into one central strategy.

## BLOCKS TO GETTING IT DONE: A REVIEW

Your procrastination problem is probably like a mulligan stew. It has its own ingredients. While some of these ingredients might be like everybody else's, the specific configuration of your problem is unique. Your unique procrastination problem can be mild or severe or sometimes mild and sometimes severe. Your problem may be a mildly annoying habit that gets in the way of productivity but that can be readily overcome. Or your problem may represent severe inhibitions and emotional restrictions that require more work to overcome—but when you start getting it done you become an emotionally freer and significantly more productive and happier you.

Your unique procrastination problem is usually (but not always) the result of multiple causes. For example, it can be the result of observing and imitating people who procrastinate. The problem can develop because you have a proclivity for seeking comfort and for avoiding activities that appear unpleasant. Procrastination can also develop because you adhere to a false assumption that you can't be a worthy person unless you are a super person.

When you think your worth as a person depends upon continuously gaining approval or turning in perfect performances, you run a high risk of procrastinating out of fear of not achieving such impossible goals. Thus, if you believe, unfortunately, that you must act superbly but in fact act as if you believed it is better to procrastinate than to be found wrong or imperfect, you lock yourself into a no-win situation. The consequences of this situation are generally twofold: You fear failure and so avoid acting; you defame yourself for this inactivity.

Some strive to surmount these no-win situations by developing such solutions as blaming the world or attempting to stop feeling altogether. When these extreme tactics fail, troubles are typically compounded: You anguish over your inability to control the external world; you anguish over your inability to let go and enjoy life.

To avoid compounding troubles, a person who procrastinates often tries to make excuses and to deceive himself into believing that all is well when it is not. Unfortunately, when this attitude is a dominant way of coping, procrastination problems are perpetuated. The reason problems are perpetuated is because words are imaginatively used to magically cloak reality. The human capacity for imaginatively twisting meaning is used in the service of motives to avoid self-detection. By allowing this imaginative excuse-making side to dominate, one distorts reality and easily becomes immobilized. Some have described this as "immobilization in a teardrop."

This process of immobilization has its foundations in still other aspects of your life. Immobilization can be the result of psychological inhibitions regarding participation in new ventures. It can be a manifestation of an attempt to insulate oneself from a too-readily triggered tendency to believe that the "emotional pain" of facing a conflict will be too excruciating.

Procrastination may represent a conflict in values, and, for example, be solidly tied to failure to identify and to act in congruence with your own basic values. For instance, you may think that you value having an adequate income as well as leisure time in which to spend it. You may also think that you must hold onto your job at all costs because you'll never get another one as good. So you compulsively involve yourself in working excessive hours to avoid losing your job (avoid failure) and then have a miserable time because you've thwarted your own value for having fun. Your security needs dominate and frustrate your other needs and values. As is the case of the frustrated artist, your focus is upon survival rather than on living.

# AWARENESS AND ACTION:
# THE PATHWAY TO LIVING

Whether your problem is mulitfaceted (typical) or the result of a single pivotal experience (less likely), to get it done you will have to put forth effort to change. It is the theme of this book that it is not enough to be aware of your problem and to be aware of ways of changing. You have to begin to act the way you would like to act if you want to do better.

Awareness is not sufficient unto itself to promote change. Your awareness of your procrastination problem, however, and the strategies you can initiate to come to terms with your problem can now be organized into a comprehensive, result-centered action plan.

In the remainder of this chapter I intend to illustrate how you can develop such a plan. The system used to establish the plan is analytic, cognitive, and behavioral. It is analytic in the sense that the approach requires you to employ your reasoning powers and to look for evidence to identify the basis of your problem and clarify its ramifications. It is cognitive in that the approach requires that you work to restructure your thinking to conform to a non-excuse-making, objective outlook. It is behavioral in that it requires that you act to change. As you integrate all three overlapping strategies, you help yourself to stop procrastinating.

This result-centered awareness-action approach combines techniques previously described. I present them in a format to help you to *identify* your problem, *organize* your thinking, and *focus* upon self-help methods. This method involves honest reflection and work to implement. But if you are conscientious in this effort, you will save yourself considerable time!

To help you use this method I will describe a case of a person with a self-development procrastination problem who used this particular result-centered method to organize her battle against procrastination.

The person is Joan, a thirty-two-year-old bookkeeper with a

history of inadequacy feelings and procrastination. Joan was the youngest of five children. Her father died shortly after she was born. As she grew up she was ashamed of her mother's broken English and lack of education.

During her school years, Joan withdrew from contacts with other children and invested her time in her studies. She dated very infrequently and after high school entered a two-year college and obtained an associate's degree in bookkeeping.

Joan's major self-development problem was centered on her interpersonal interactions. Despite her expressed desire to have friends, her fear of rejection was so great that she usually avoided people. Furthermore, when she dated (rarely) she would select men to whom she was not attracted. Indeed, if any man she dated showed an interest in her, she would stop dating him. She seemed to be living by Groucho Marx's comment that he wouldn't belong to any club that would have him as a member: She wasn't interested in men who were interested in her. She felt too inadequate to try to relate to men she found attractive.

In addition to her problem with men, Joan was petrified to go to lunch with her coworkers, afraid of joining a bridge club, and so on. She thought she was too inept to bang a nail into the wall, flooded herself with invectives, felt humiliated over her flaws, panicked over feeling tense, became tense and impatient if hassled or inconvenienced, and so forth. Although these problems were hardly fatal, they resulted in much misery and suffering.

The suffering Joan experienced was what motivated her to enter therapy. Through therapy she hoped to get rid of all emotional pain. She also wanted to grow as a person and enjoy life more. She was, however, very resistant to the proposition of changing her self-defeating attitude and self-restrictive ways. She wanted to develop her positive personal qualities, but procrastinated doing the very things that would help her to develop.

After I helped Joan to see what her self-defeating patterns were and how they evolved, we decided to develop a self-monitoring plan that would help her take initial steps toward improving her self-image, fostering better interpersonal relations, and tolerating tension.

As you can imagine, after many years of involvement in faulty thinking and acting patterns Joan had many more problems than this initial program suggests. For example, she had a major authority hang-up. Part of her problem with men resulted from selecting men who were like her mother—men she could not respect. At a deeper level, her "lack of respect" for her mother was a defensive reaction to the hurt feelings associated with the belief that she did not get enough love and affection from her. Thus, she feared getting hurt if she became intimate with a man whose love she wanted.

Joan's job did not parallel her interests, and so she would merely go through the work routine with great aversion. She worked hard, however, so as to avoid incurring the wrath of her boss.

To help Joan overcome procrastinating, we worked to develop a *result-centered awareness action plan* following this sequence:

1. Paper and pencil were obtained.
2. The paper was turned sideways.
3. The sheet was divided into three major columns: "Basic Problem," "Problem Manifestations," and "Action Plan."
4. Under "Basic Problem," we identified three problems Joan most strongly wanted to minimize (poor self-image, excessive approval seeking, and intolerance for tension—see the table on pages 189 and 190).
5. In the second column, we identified how these problems were manifested in her daily life.
6. In the third column, we developed action-plan strategies to attack the procrastination problems and their manifestations.
7. We developed a separate chart so that Joan could record her progress.
8. We assigned numerical weighting to each activity, based upon difficulty level.
9. Each time Joan completed an action-plan activity, she re-

corded the activity and the appropriate number of points in a notebook she carried with her at all times.

10. At the end of each week she tallied up the total number of points for each action-plan activity and recorded them on a cumulative graph. (The table, the chart, and the graph follow the text at the end of this chapter.) The way the graph procedure works is: (a) Add each new weekly point count to the point counts of the previous weeks; (b) Put a dot on the chart equal to the total number of points (vertical axis) over the week you are summarizing (horizontal axis); (c) Connect the dots from week to week.

In the development of the plan, we used pattern analysis and a modification of the charting procedure.

Joan continued in therapy while working on her plan. She systematically followed the plan, relying on a wide variety of follow-through strategies to help. For example, she employed extrinsic rewards, rewarding herself by eating at her favorite restaurant each time she accumulated sixty points. She employed the five-minute system to help her continue using rational-emotive therapy techniques for eliminating belittling self-statements. She used positive imagery to help herself develop a positive outlook and ask colleagues to lunch, ask men questions, and act friendly and enthusiastically.

As an intrinsic reward for her efforts, Joan found herself becoming more adventuresome and consistently enjoying life. She began to feel a surge of self-confidence, a feeling she had rarely experienced before.

Try developing your own integrated-awareness action plan. Use the format that Joan used for a start.

In the next chapter I will describe what your life could be like once you've effectively organized and directed your efforts and kicked the procrastination habit.

## PROBLEM ANALYSIS

| Basic Problem | Problem Manifestations | Action Plans |
|---|---|---|
| I. Poor Self-Image | I. Poor Self-Image | I. Self-Acceptance |
| | A. Faulty self-labeling | A. Defusing feelings of worthlessness |
| |   1. defines self as unattractive |   1. Identify belittling self-statements. |
| |   2. calls self stupid, inadequate, no good |   2. Consider constructive alternatives to these belittling self-statements. |
| | |   3. Try to see yourself through compassionate eyes. |
| | |   4. Prove to yourself that you're not a total loser. |
| | B. Faulty forecasting | B. Improving forecasting |
| |   1. predicts failure for performances |   1. Consider 5 positive outcomes for each worrisome situation. |
| |   2. predicts inability to change |   2. Imagine coping effectively. |
| |   3. anticipates worst possible outcome—anxiety and depressed feelings |   3. Try to act the way you'd like to feel and think. |
| II. Fear of Disapproval | II. Fear of Disapproval | II. Positive Approval Seeking |
| | A. avoids going to lunch with colleagues | A. Take a colleague to lunch twice a week. |
| | B. avoids approaching attractive men | B. Ask 5 attractive men per week for exact time. |
| | C. fails to express opinions | C. Express 2 opinions per day to a different colleague or acquaintance. |
| | D. dodges old acquaintances | D. Call at least 1 acquaintance per week. |
| | E. isolates self on weekends | E. Plan and carry through an activity each weekend. |

189

# PROBLEM ANALYSIS (cont.)

| Basic Problem | Problem Manifestations | Action Plans |
|---|---|---|
| | F. acts cool and aloof | F. Try to act friendly by greeting people each day, by smiling and saying, "Hello." |
| | G. acts unenthusiastic | G. Express enthusiasm by telling someone about an experience that you enjoyed. |
| III. Comfort Seeking | III. Comfort Seeking | III. Tolerance Building |
| | A. Invents excuses to dodge uncomfortable situations | A. Eliminating excuse making |
| |   1. Where you may be tested |   1. Identify typical excuses—"I'm too tired"; "I won't know enough." |
| |   2. Making new social contacts |   2. Try to catch yourself using these excuses *and* |
| | |   3. Convince yourself that you can act even though tired or less well prepared than desired. |
| | |   4. Act. |
| | B. Fearful of feeling tense | B. Learning to bear discomfort |
| | |   1. Allow self to experience discomfort. |
| | |   2. Ask self: If you were getting paid $100 for each minute of mental anguish, how long could you stand it? |
| | C. Tries to follow familiar routines, avoids risks | C. Try 2 productive activities per week that are novel, risky, or uncomfortable. |
| | D. Feels strong sense of impatience when slightly inconvenienced, having to wait | D. Try to figure out why you can't tolerate being inconvenienced or having to wait. |

190

# PROGRESS CHART

| SELF-ACCEPTANCE | SEPT. 5 | SEPT. 12 | SEPT. 17 | SEPT. 24 | OCT. 1 | OCT. 7 |
|---|---|---|---|---|---|---|
| ● QUESTION BELITTLING STATEMENTS (1) | 5 | 10 | 13 | 25 | 15 | 20 |
| ● CONSIDER CONSTRUCTIVE ALTERNATIVES (1) | 3 | 5 | 2 | 10 | 10 | 10 |
| ● POSITIVE SELF-VIEW (1) | 1 | 2 | 5 | 10 | 5 | 10 |
| ● CONSIDER 5 POSITIVE OUTCOMES (1) | 6 | 5 | 5 | 10 | 10 | 5 |
| ● IMAGINE COPING EFFECTIVELY (1) | | 3 | 5 | 10 | 5 | 10 |
| ● ACT THE WAY YOU'D LIKE TO FEEL (1) | 1 | 2 | 5 | 10 | 5 | 10 |
| **POSITIVE APPROVAL-SEEKING** | | | | | | |
| ● TAKE A COLLEAGUE TO LUNCH (5) | 5 | 5 | 10 | 10 | 15 | 20 |
| ● ASK MEN QUESTIONS (5) | 5 | 5 | 5 | | 10 | |
| ● EXPRESS 2 OPINIONS (2) | | 2 | 4 | | 10 | |
| ● CALL ACQUAINTANCE (2) | | | 6 | | 4 | |
| ● PLAN AND FOLLOW THROUGH (5) | | 5 | 10 | 10 | 5 | 15 |
| ● ACTING FRIENDLY (1) | | 1 | | | 1 | 5 |
| ● EXPRESS ENTHUSIASM (1) | 1 | 1 | 1 | | 5 | 5 |
| **TOLERANCE BUILDING** | | | | | | |
| ● ELIMINATING EXCUSES (2) | 2 | 2 | 4 | | 10 | 20 |
| ● BEARING DISCOMFORT (5) | | 5 | 10 | 5 | 5 | 10 |
| ● NOVEL RISK-TAKING (5) | | | 6 | | 5 | 10 |
| ● TOLERATING INCONVENIENCE (2) | 2 | 2 | | | | |
| TOTAL | 30 | 50 | 90 | 100 | 120 | 150 |
| CUMULATIVE TOTALS | | 80 | 170 | 270 | 390 | 540 |

# PROGRESS GRAPH

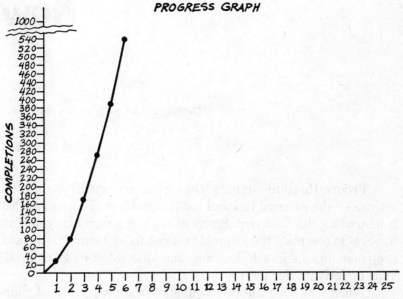

# 1ɔ

# Self-fulfillment
# Through
# Doing
# t
# Now

"Getting it done really can be more fun."

Procrastination signals that you are putting off two activities—the external task and the internal task of changing what is motivating this behavior. Procrastination is a signal for you both to begin to complete the external task and to try to understand and overcome the basic self-doubting and discomfort-dodging problems underlying this pattern.

When you heed the procrastination warning, you lead yourself into actions that make your life more orderly and pave the way for moving away from fearing discomfort and failure and toward spontaneity. With this freedom comes the urge to follow your own curiosities and to test your abilities so as to discover the person you really are. By following your own natural inclinations for getting it done, you come to enjoy life more because you have more time to live, learn, and experience pleasure.

Whereas you can make great gains in shrinking a procrastination problem, you can never beat the problem completely, totally, and for all time. Some procrastination is normal. It is only when the problem is pervasive that you are in serious trouble. Therefore, expect that from time to time you will procrastinate. However, by accepting that this problem will periodically occur, you won't expect yourself to be perfect and then end up experiencing anxiety when you slip up and put off. Instead, recognize that it is important to continue efforts in getting it done to prevent this problem from spreading like a malaise.

The recognition that you are progressing in your campaign of getting it done and that this is a lifetime process helps you to rid yourself of the myth that a one-time campaign to stop procrastinating will climax in one final magnificent victory. Moreover, when you work at being better organized and prompt, you are less likely to feel guilty because you believe you are letting yourself or others down because of your delays.

Feelings of worthlessness and guilt fuel procrastination. By getting it done you will experience these feelings less and less and therefore will tend to put less off. You will be less centered on your problems and therefore more objective in your outlook. When you are more objective, you will tend to act in your best interests. Consequently, you are less likely to be a victim of your own procrastination and experience guilt because of it.

This objective outlook has other major advantages. One chief advantage is an ability to realistically estimate the time and effort it will take to complete a project. This estimation means that you will be able to utilize your time to maximum advantage. As an antiprocrastinator, you will accomplish more in less time than your procrastinating colleagues. You will, in fact, maximize your competency as you advantageously and effectively utilize your time.

As a successful antiprocrastinator you'll experience less tension because you will have less to be tense about. Experiencing less tension, you will require more than a normal amount of stress to overreact, and so you will overreact less. Thus your judgment will be clearer and better when you are faced with tough decisions. You therefore will be making better decisions concerning how to deal with hassles and how to advance yourself.

When you competently contend with the details of living, you will find your style of living to be more relaxed. Your timing and pacing will be better, and you will be more open to your experiences.

Instead of worrying about what you haven't done, your sensory experiences will replace the worry and will be pleasurably heightened as you become freer to concentrate your attention on to them. For example, you'll likely enjoy your meals more because you pay attention to the good taste of your food. When you lie on the beach, you will fully enjoy the warmth of the sun and the smell of the fresh salt air. You'll generally feel more alive and experience life as increasingly more fulfilling once you have freed yourself of the worry, guilt, and depression over what you have put off or are fearful of doing.

As an antiprocrastinator, you'll be less defensive, because you will have less to be defensive about. You won't have to excuse or justify your delays with the same regularity as when you procrastinate. Therefore, you will avoid the acute sense of discomfort you typically experience when you try to give excuses for delaying. Your interpersonal relationships will probably improve as a result of your new-found ability to be realistic and honest. That is because you will have little to cover up and so can afford to authentically be yourself.

# Bibliography

The following references discuss concepts that are relevant to understanding procrastination or describe procedures that can be translated into an antiprocrastination action program. Since there is a dearth of information currently existing under the title "procrastination," only a few of the following references mention or refer to it. Those that do are so designated with an asterisk (*). However, as I have defined procrastination, most references present ideas that can be adapted for understanding and solving the problem. These references that I believe to be of the most practical value are marked with a bullet (•).

**Abramson, L. Y., Seligman, E. P., & Teasdale, J. D.** Learned helplessness in humans: Critique and reformulation. *Journal of Abnormal Psychology*, 1978, 87, 49–74.

●**Adams, N.** This year we've got to get organized. *Chicago Magazine*, January 1978, 104–13.

●*\*Adler, A.* *Understanding human behavior*. New York: Fawcett World, 1974.

**Alberti, R. E., & Emmons, M. L.** *Your perfect right*. San Luis Obispo, Ca.: Impact, 1974.

**Assagioli, R.** *Psychosynthesis*. New York: Viking, 1971.

**Ausubel, D. P.** *The psychology of meaningful verbal learning*. New York: Grune and Stratton, 1963.

**Atkinson, J. W., & Litwin, G. H.** Achievement motivation and test anxiety conceived as motive to approach success and to avoid failure. *Journal of Abnormal and Social Psychology*, 1960, *60*, 52–63.

*\*Bach, G. R., & Goldberg, H.** *Creative aggression*. New York: Doubleday & Company, 1974.

**Bandura, A.** *Principles of behavioral modification*. New York: Holt, Rinehart & Winston, 1969.

**Beck, A. T.** *Depression: Clinical, experimental, and theoretical aspects*. New York: Hoeber, 1967.

●**Beck, A. T.** *Cognitive therapy and the emotional disorders*. New York: International Universities Press, 1976.

●**Bem, D.** Self-perception theory. In Berkowitz (Ed.) *Advances in experimental social psychology* (Vol. 6). New York: Academic Press, 1972, 1–62.

●**Bois, J.** *The art of awareness*. Dubuque, Iowa: W. C. Brown, 1966.

**Brown, W. F., & Holtzman, W. H.** *Survey of study habits and attitudes*. New York: The Psychological Corp., 1966.

Coates, T. J., & Thoresen, C. E. *How to sleep better*. Englewood Cliffs, New Jersey: Prentice-Hall, Inc., 1977.

*Dell, D. M. Counselor power base, influence attempt, and behavioral change in counseling. *Journal of Counseling Psychology*, 1973, *20*, 399–405.

*Dewey, J. *Moral principles in education*. New York: Houghton Mifflin Co., 1909.

Dewey, J. *The child and the curriculum and the school and society*. Chicago: University of Chicago Press, 1971.

●Dunlap, K. *Habits: Their making and unmaking*. New York: Liveright, 1972.

●Ellis, A. *Reason and emotion in psychotherapy*. New York: Lyle Stuart, 1962.

●Ellis, A., & Harper, R. A. *A new guide to rational living*. Englewood Cliffs, New Jersey: Prentice-Hall, Inc., and Hollywood Wilshire Books, 1975.

●*Ellis, A., & Knaus, W. J. *Overcoming procrastination*. New York: Rational Living, 1977.

Evans, R. I. *Carl Rogers: The man and his ideas*. New York: Dutton, 1975.

Fagan, J., & Shepard, I. C. *Gestalt therapy now*. Palo Alto, Ca.: Science and Behavioral Books, 1970.

Farley, F. H. Individual differences in examination persistence and performance. *The Journal of Educational Research*, 1974, *67*, 344–6.

Farrelly, F., & Brandsma, J. *Provocative therapy*. Fort Collins, Col.: Shields Publishing, 1974.

Fay, A. *Making things better by making them worse*. New York: Hawthorne Books, 1978.

Feather, N. T. Attribution of responsibility and balance of success and failure in relation to initial confidence and task performance. *Journal of Personality and Social Psychology*, 1969, *13*, 129–44.

**Frankl, V. E.** *The doctor and the soul*. New York: Vintage Books, 1973.

●**Frankl, V.E.** Paradoxical intention and dereflexion. *Psychotherapy, Theory, Research, and Practice*, 1975, *12*, 226–36.

●**Freud, A.** *The ego and the mechanisms of defense*. New York: International Universities Press, 1946.

**Freud, S.** *Beyond the pleasure principle* (standard edition). London: Hogarth Press, 1955.

**Gagné, R. M.** *The conditions of learning*. New York: Holt, Rinehart & Winston, 1965.

**Gerard, H. B.** Emotional uncertainty and social comparison, *Journal of Abnormal and Social Psychology*, 1963, *66*, 568–73.

**Glass, D. C., Canavan, D., & Schiavo, S.** Achievement motivation, dissonance, and defensiveness. *Journal of Personality*, 1968, *36*, 474–92.

●**Glasser, W.** *Reality therapy, a new approach to psychiatry*. New York: Harper and Row, 1965.

**Goldfried, M., & Davidson, G.** *Clinical behavioral therapy*. New York: Holt, Rinehart & Winston, 1976.

●**Haley, J.** *Problem solving therapy*. San Francisco: Jossey Bass, 1976.

**Haley, J.** *Uncommon psychotherapy*. New York: Ballantine Books, 1973.

**Hartman, H.** *Ego psychology and the problem of adaptation*. New York: International Universities Press, 1968.

**Hayakawa, S. I.** *Language in thought and action* (rev. edition). New York: Harcourt, Brace & World, 1964.

**Heider F.** *The psychology of interpersonal relations*. New York: John Wiley & Sons, 1958.

●**Herzberg, A.** *Active psychotherapy*. New York: Grune and Stratton, 1945.

Horney, K. *The neurotic personality of our times*. New York: Norton, 1937.

Horney, K. *Neurosis and human growth*. New York: Norton, 1950.

Huesmann, L. R. (Ed.). Special issue: Learned helplessness: A model of depression. *Journal of Abnormal Psychology*, 1978, 87, 1–198.

Jacobson, E. *You must relax*. New York: Whittlesey House, 1934.

James, W. *Psychology*. New York: Holt, 1892.

●James, W. *Talks to teachers on psychology: And to students on some of life ideals*. New York: Holt, 1906.

Johnson, W. *People in quandries*. New York: Harper & Row, 1946.

Jones, E. C., Kanouse, D. E., Kelly, H. H., Nisbett, R. E., Valins, S., & Weiner, B. *Attribution: Perceiving the causes of behavior*. New York: General Learning Press, 1972.

Kanfer, F. H. Self-monitoring: Methodological limitations and clinical applications. *Journal of Consulting and Clinical Psychology*, 1970, 35, 148–52.

●Kazdin, A. E. Self-monitoring and behavior change. In Mahoney, M. J., & Thorensen, C. E., *Self control: Power to the person*. Monterey, Ca.: Brooks-Cole, 1974, 218–46.

Kelly, G. *The psychology of personal constructs: A theory of personality* (Vol 1). New York: Norton, 1955.

●Kelley, H. H. The process of causal attribution. *American Psychologist*, 1973, 28, 107–28.

Knaus, W. J. *Rational-emotive education*. New York: Institute for Rational Living Press, 1974.

●*Knaus, W. J. Overcoming Procrastination. *Rational Living*, 1973, 8, 2–7.

●Knaus, W. J., & Wessler, R. L. Rational emotive problem simulation. *Rational Living*, 1976, 11, 8–11.

**Korman, A. K.** Task success, task popularity, and self-esteem as influence on task liking. *Journal of Applied Psychology*, 1968, 52, 484–90.

**Korzypski, A.** *Science and sanity*. Lakeville, Conn.: International Non-Aristolean Library, 1958 (4th edition).

**Kris, E.** *The psychology of caricature: Psychoanalytic explorations in art*. New York: International Universities Press, 1952.

●\*Lakein, A. L.** *How to get control of your time and your life*. New York: Peter Wyden, 1973.

●**Lazarus, A. A.** *Behavior therapy and beyond*. New York: McGraw-Hill, 1971.

**Lazarus, A. A.** *Multi-modal therapy*. New York: Springer, 1976.

**Lazarus, R. S.** *Psychological stress and the coping processes*. New York: McGraw-Hill, 1966.

**Leonard, S., & Weitz, J.** Task enjoyment and task perseverence in relation to task success and self esteem. *Journal of Applied Psychology*, 1971, 5, 414–21.

**Levine, J.** Information seeking with conflicting and irrelevant imputs. *Journal of Applied Psychology*, 1973, 57, 74–80.

●**Low, A. A.** *Mental health through will training*. Boston: The Christopher Publishing House, 1950.

**Maher, B.** *Clinical psychology and personality: The selected papers of George Kelly*. New York: John Wiley & Sons, 1969.

**Mahoney, M. J.** *Cognition and behavior modification*. Cambridge: Ballinger, 1974.

●**Mahoney, M. J., & Thorensen, C. E.** *Self-control, power to the person*. Monterey, Ca.: Brooks-Cole, 1974.

**Maltz, M.** *Psycho-cybernetics: A new way to get more living out of life*. Englewood Cliffs, New Jersey: Prentice-Hall, 1960.

**Mandler, G.** The interruption of behavior. In Levine, D. (Ed.), *Nebraska symposium on motivation*. Lincoln: University of Nebraska Press, 1964, 163–219.

Mandler, G., & Watson, D. L.   Anxiety and the interruption of behavior. In Spielberger, C. (Ed.), *Anxiety and behavior*. New York: Academic Press, 1966, 263–88.

McClelland, D. C.   *The achievement motive*. New York: Appleton-Century-Crofts, 1953.

Meichenbaum, D.   *Cognitive-behavior modification*. Morristown, N. J.: General Learning Press, 1974.

●Meichenbaum, D.   *Cognitive-behavior modification*. New York: Plenum Press, 1978.

Meir, E. I.   Relationship between intrinsic needs and women's persistance at work. *Journal of Applied Psychology*, 1972, *56*, 293–6.

Mischel, W.   *Personality and assessment*. New York: John Wiley & Sons, 1968.

Moreno, J. L.   *Psychodrama*. New York: Beacon, 1946.

Murray, H. A.   American Icarus. In Burton, A., & Harris, R. E. (Eds.). *Clinical studies in personality*. New York: Harper & Row, 1955.

Nickerson, R. S., & Feeher, C. E.   Decision making and training: A review of theoretical and empirical studies on decision making and their implication for the training of decision makers. *Catalog of Selected Documents in Psychology*, 1977, 7, 50–71.

Nisbett, R. E., & Valins, S.   *Perceiving the cause of one's own behavior*. New York: General Learning Press, 1971.

Ouspensky, D. D.   *The psychology of man's possible evolution*. New York: Knopf, 1954.

●Perls, F., Hefferline, R. F., & Goodman, P.   *Gestalt therapy*. New York: Julian Press, 1951.

Perls, F. C.   *Gestalt therapy verbatim*. Lafayette, Ca.: Real People's Press, 1969.

Rimm, D. C., & Masters, J. C., *Behavior therapy*. New York: Academic Press, 1974.

**Potter, S.** *One-upmanship.* New York: Henry Holt, 1952.

**Premack, D.** Reinforcement theory. In Levene, D. (Ed.), *Nebraska symposium on motivation.* Lincoln, Neb.: University of Nebraska Press, 1965.

\***Ringenbeck, P. T.** *Procrastination throughout the ages: A definitive history.* Palmer Lake, Col.: Filter Press, 1971.

●**Rogers, C. L.** *On Becoming a person.* Boston: Houghton Mifflin, 1961.

**Salter, A.** *Conditioned reflex therapy.* New York: Creative Age Press, 1949.

**Schachter, S., & Singer, J. E.** Cognitive, social, and physiological determinents of emotional state. *Psychological Review,* 1962, *69,* 374–99.

●**Shelton, J. L., & Ackerman, J. M.** *Homework in counseling and psychotherapy.* Springfield, Ill.: Thomas, 1974.

\***Sieveking, N. A., Campbell, M. L., Rileigh, W. J., & Savitsky, J.** Mass intervention by mail for an academic impediment. *Journal of Consulting and Clinical Psychology,* 1971, *18,* 601–2.

**Skinner, B. F.** *Science and human behavior.* New York: Macmillan, 1953.

**Skinner, B. F.** *About behaviorism.* New York: Knopf, 1974.

**Snygg, D., & Combs, A. W.** *Individual behavior.* New York: Harper, 1949.

**Strub, M.** Experience and prior probability in a complex decision task. *Journal of Applied Psychology,* 1969, *53,* 112–17.

**Stuart, R. B., & Davis, B.** *Slim chance in a fat world: Behavioral control of obesity.* Champaign, Ill.: Research Press, 1972.

**Thorensen, C. E., & Mahoney, M.** *Behavioral self-control.* New York: Holt, Rinehart & Winston, 1974.

**Thorndike, E. L.** *The fundamentals of learning.* New York: Teachers College, 1932.

Thorndike, E. L. *The psychology of wants, interests, and attitudes*. New York: Appleton-Century, 1935.

Watson, J. B. Psychology as the behaviorist views it. *Psychological Review*, 1913, *20*, 158–77.

Watson, J. B. *Psychology from the standpoint of a behaviorist*. Philadelphia: Lippincott, 1919.

●Weinberg, H. H. *Levels of knowing and existence: Studies in general semantics*. New York: Harper & Row, 1959.

Weiner, B., Frieze, I., Kukla, A., Reed, L., Rest, S. A., & Rosenbaum, R. M. *Perceiving the causes of success and failure*. New York: General Learning Press, 1971.

*Wessman, A. Personality and the subjective experience of time. *Journal of Personality Assessment*. 1973, 37, 103–14.

●Wolpe, J. *The practice of behavior therapy*. New York: Pergamon Press, 1969.

●Wolpe, J., & Lazarus, A. A. *Behavior therapy techniques*. New York: Pergamon Press, 1966.

# Index

Reward, 155–58, 160–65
Risk taking, 120
Rogers, Carl, 136–37
Role-playing techniques, 104–6
Rushing, 87–88

## S

Self-cons, 20–33, 48
Self-control program, 154–69
Self-doubt, 4, 6–8, 78, 82, 137
Self-downing, 6, 82
Sensitivity, maladjusted, 135
Sensory-appreciation exercises, 50
Set-go technique, 152–53
"Should I or shouldn't I?" debate, 22–23
Shyness, 69–73
Skinner, B. F., 155
Stop-check technique, 103
Stratagem, 4
Switchover technique, 24–25

## T

Tension, 32, 58, 59, 83, 87, 109–10
Thorensen, Carl, 155
Thorndike, Edward, 155
Time-saving strategies, 146–48
Trust, 43

## U

Unknown, fear of, 123–24

## V

Vindictive perfectionism, 56–59

## W

Wait:
  hating to, 87–88
  learning to, 88–90
Watson, John, 155
Work-aholism, 7, 21

4423